1 MONTH OF
FREE
READING

at

www.ForgottenBooks.com

By purchasing this book you are
eligible for one month membership to
ForgottenBooks.com, giving you
unlimited access to our entire
collection of over 1,000,000 titles via
our web site and mobile apps.

To claim your free month visit:

www.forgottenbooks.com/free927083

ISBN 978-0-260-08878-9
PIBN 10927083

This book is a reproduction of an important historical work. Forgotten Books uses
state-of-the-art technology to digitally reconstruct the work, preserving the original format
whilst repairing imperfections present in the aged copy. In rare cases, an imperfection in
the original, such as a blemish or missing page, may be replicated in our edition. We do,
however, repair the vast majority of imperfections successfully; any imperfections that
remain are intentionally left to preserve the state of such historical works.

FISCAL YEARS 1948 AND 1949

Like our aims
Thy tower stands
So high

Presented to the Library
The State Teachers College
at Towson
by

A Foundation

OF THE

BOARD OF SCHOOL COMMISSIONERS

OF BALTIMORE CITY
TO THE
MAYOR AND CITY COUNCIL

JULY 1, 1948 TO JUNE 30, 1950
AND THE
FISCAL YEARS 1948 AND 1949

TABLE OF CONTENTS

489707

BOARD OF SCHOOL COMMISSIONERS

(As of June 30, 1950)

OFFICERS

Educational Direction

Business Management

LETTER OF TRANSMITTAL

BALTIMORE, MD., JUNE 30, 1950

HONORABLE THOMAS D'ALESANDRO, JR.,

Mayor of Baltimore

Dear Mr. Mayor:

The accompanying report, the One Hundred and Nineteenth in the entire series of reports by the Board of School Commissioners, covers a two-year period ending June 30, 1950, and embracing the two school years, 1948-1949 and 1949-1950.

During this biennium Baltimore has been fortunate in having on the School Board an exceedingly able and devoted group of men and women who have given freely of their time and energy to the consideration of problems of policy that affect thousands of students and teachers in the public school system. The membership of the Board has remained almost unchanged throughout the entire period, and the resulting cumulative experience and understanding of the problems of a large school system have been most beneficial to the system as a whole.

The Department has enjoyed the confidence of the public. At the election held on November 2, 1948, overwhelming approval was given for the final $1,000,000 of the $3,000,000 School Equipment Loan approved in May, 1947. These funds have made possible replacement of many obsolete tools of teaching, and have in some cases provided a supply where none existed before. Classroom and library furniture and books, playground and gymnasium equipment, typewriters and office machines, lockers, art, music, science, health and vocational equipment, are a vital part of today's school.

In the major program of providing new school plants, and improvement in existing inadequate buildings, the most important achievement has been the emphasis upon a master plan that attempts to identify the needs of the city as a whole, with due attention to cyclic waves of enrollment, the shifts of population within the city, the trends in births, and similar facts. These are the foundation upon which adequate plans must rest.

Meanwhile the instructional program—the soul of any school—has been strengthened in countless ways by widespread professional activity within the teaching force. Much of this strong professional interest has been the direct result of the participation of over 3,500 teachers in professional courses, committees, and workshops.

On behalf of the members of the Board of School Commissioners and of the staff, I extend to you and to the Board of Estimates, the City Council, and the citizens of Baltimore, our appreciation of the generous and understanding support which has been given the Board in its endeavors to advance the program of public education in Baltimore.

Respectfully submitted,

ROSZEL C. THOMSEN,
President, Board of School Commissioners

To the Board of School Commissioners,
Baltimore, Maryland.

Dr. Morrissy, Mrs. Rysanek, and Gentlemen:

In accordance with Article II, Section 9, of the Rules,
I respectfully present the accompanying report on the development of the public schools of Baltimore during the
two scholastic years ending June 30, 1949, and June 30,
1950, constituting the One Hundred Nineteenth Report of
the Department of Education.

It is recognized today, more clearly than ever, that the
success of an enterprise must be measured not only in the
appropriateness and quality of the service rendered or in
the timeliness and value of the goods produced, but also
in its effect upon the people who participate in it. The
success of an industry, a newspaper, a college, or a public
school system is dependent upon releasing and developing
the latent abilities and creative energies of its entire staff.
In a school system every person should have the opportunity to contribute both in his own immediate position, and
in the formation of general policy. This concept of good
administration has guided our efforts in Baltimore. No
more eloquent testimony could be given to the responsive-
ness of our principals and teachers than the fact that each
year, in addition to the regular duties which all perform,
over 3000 individuals have served on committees or have
participated in courses or workshops to find ways of making
themselves better educational leaders of children and adults.

The educational progress shown in this report could not
have been achieved without the cooperation of thousands
of citizens and parents, the Governor, the Mayor, members
of the Board of Estimates, legislators, and City Council-
men, who recognize the need for improved educational
opportunities for Baltimore's children. Many civic organizations, private educational institutions, and thousands of
individual laymen have contributed to our work. The
press, radio, television, and cinema have also assisted by

informing the public of what the schools are doing. Our best information medium has and will always be the children and their parents.

The report itself is prepared from the material supplied by the members of the Department of Education staff, including the Superintendent of Schools, the Assistant Superintendents, the Directors, and the Assistant Directors of various departments, the Supervisors, and Assistant Supervisors of grades and special subjects, and the Bureau of Research. Dr. Harold B. Chapman, Assistant Director of Research, had editorial supervision of the entire report. It is due to his diligence and efficiency that the data were assembled in a unified report. To the present members of the Board of School Commissioners, and to Mr. George W. F. McMechen, whose term expired during the biennium, I wish to express my own sincere appreciation for the able, unstinted, and statesmanlike service they have rendered to the cause of public education in our city, state, and nation.

I personally appreciate the understanding cooperation and assistance you have given me during this period. In serving as a legislative body, passing upon and adopting educational policies, you have acted in accordance with the best thought in educational administration throughout the country.

Sincerely yours,

WILLIAM H. LEMMEL,
Superintendent

I

ADMINISTRATION OF SCHOOLS

The One Hundred and Nineteenth Report of the Board of School Commissioners covers the two scholastic years 1948-1949 and 1949-1950, and the fiscal years 1948, 1949, and a part of 1950. During this period the professional development program for teachers, supervisors, and others, offering a wide choice of study and practical experience through group meetings under trained leadership, not only provided a medium of fruitful growth for teachers but also produced instructional materials of great value and interest to the children under their care. The operation of the new salary schedule, which at the time of its adoption was considered among the five best in the twenty largest cities, was liberalized through new policies of accreditation and leaves of absence. New buildings were being designed or in process of erection in all parts of the city. Unmet needs for new or expanded facilities were under continuous study by the School Plant Planning Committee and the Board of School Commissioners. Through the funds supplied by the School Equipment Loan and the Building Repair Loan school buildings became more efficient and happier places of work. Finally, with the aid of thousands of parents and other laymen meeting in small and large groups with supervisors, teachers and principals, problems concerning the education of children and adults were under concerted attack on many different fronts.

Financial Support

Appropriations to the Department of Education in the annual budgets for the fiscal years 1949 and 1950 provided larger amounts from the general tax levy than in former years, and capital replacement and improvement funds from the several school loans. These appropriations are given in detail in Table 1. They reflect the new salary schedule which was adopted in 1947 and made fully effective on January 1, 1949, provision for additional teachers in elementary schools to reduce class size and to meet the

9

needs for a fast growing enrollment of pupils, and a limited expansion of services to pupils and teachers. They were also unique in their generous provisions for overcom-

TABLE 1

DEPARTMENT OF EDUCATION BUDGET

Nature of Appropriation	1949	1950
Total Levy and Loan Fund Appropriations	$39,324,001.50	$27,745,171.83
Budget, Ordinary Operations (Tax Levy)	22,824,001.50	23,745,171.83
Salaries	19,608,913.50	20,620,820.73
Supplies and Equipment	1,159,588.00	1,234,636.10
Operation of Buildings	751,000.00	735,500.00
Maintenance of Buildings	1,304,500.00	1,154,215.00
Loan Fund Appropriation	16,500,000.00	4,000,000.00
Sixth School Building Loan	15,000,000.00	4,000,000.00
School Equipment Loan	1,500,000.00	....

ing the huge backlog of equipment and maintenance needs that had developed as a result of insufficient appropriations in past years, accentuated by the restrictions of the war years. Expenditure of these funds provided not only the means for better teaching and more meaningful learning and long-needed improvements, but a powerful boost to the morale of teachers and pupils alike.

Aid from the State of Maryland—Since 1946 the State of Maryland, chiefly under the legislation based on the Sherbow report, has considerably enlarged its contribution to the support of Baltimore schools. Tables 2 and 3 show this trend very clearly, as well as the major sources from which school funds are derived.

In addition to its subventions for elementary and secondary schools the State of Maryland also agreed to underwrite a part of the costs of establishing a junior college in the Baltimore school system by an initial grant of $10,000 for the first school year. Later the State's contri-

TABLE 2

CONTRIBUTION OF STATE, CITY, AND OTHER SOURCES TO SCHOOL BUDGET

Year	Total Budget	State Aid [1]	Federal [2] Aid	Local Taxes	Other Sources [3]
1944	$10,835,413	$1,009,436	$ 45,953	$ 9,746,982	$ 33,042
1945	11,301,628	1,180,598	75,627	10,006,973	38,430
1946	12,286,484	1,467,085	77,327	10,695,461	46,611
1947	14,565,420	2,748,535	616,620	11,152,391	47,874
1948	18,745,099	3,792,042	269,818	14,634,503	48,736
1949	22,824,001	3,949,606	99,021	18,699,479	75,895
1950	23,745,171	4,126,124	63,389	19,450,304	105,354

[1] Includes Basic Aid, aid per classroom unit, aid for physically handicapped children, part-payment of salaries; and, in the years 1944 through 1947, aid for books and materials, for census and attendance, and high school aid; in the years 1947 through 1950, aid for Junior College.

[2] Federal Vocational Aid; and, in the years 1947 through 1950, Veterans Institute as follows:
1947 $554,496   1948 $186,950   1949 $32,973   1950 $61

[3] Includes non-resident tuition fees, School Board revenue, gate receipts from athletic events.

TABLE 3

PER CENT OF SCHOOL BUDGET DERIVED FROM STATE, CITY AND OTHER SOURCES

Year	Total Budget	State Aid	Federal Aid	Local Taxes	Other Sources
1944	100.0	9.3	0.4	90.0	0.3
1945	100.0	10.5	0.7	88.5	.3
1946	100.0	11.9	0.6	87.1	.4
1947	100.0	18.9	4.2	76.6	.3
1948	100.0	20.2	1.4	78.1	.3
1949	100.0	17.3	0.4	82.0	.3
1950	100.0	17.4	0.3	81.9	0.4

bution was enlarged and established on the basis of $100 per full-time pupil.[1] Effective July 1, 1950, the State will

[1] Under the tentative regulations adopted by the Maryland State Department of Education in September 1949, a full-time student is one who carries a program of not less than twelve semester hours. Aid is limited to Maryland residents, whether living in city or county. Pro-rata aid is provided for part-time students.

EQUIPMENT LOAN FUNDS HAVE PROVIDED THE BASIC INSTRUMENTS
NEEDED TO GIVE MUSICAL BALANCE TO BANDS AND ORCHESTRAS. MANY
PARENTS CANNOT AFFORD THE FINANCIAL RISK OF PURCHASING IN-
STRUMENTS UNTIL THEIR CHILDREN DISCOVER WHETHER OR NOT THEY
HAVE SUFFICIENT INTEREST AND TALENT TO PURSUE INSTRUMENTAL
MUSIC. SCHOOL-OWNED INSTRUMENTS ARE HELPING CHILDREN IN THIS
EXPLORATORY PERIOD

relieve the City of Baltimore of the cost of training teachers for its colored schools, a function which the city has maintained since the establishment of the first training classes in the curriculum of the Colored High School in 1901.

Baltimore City still does not participate in the State Equalization Fund, although it was the only unit of the State in June 1950 which was outside of the fund. Since education is a state function, and in view of the mobility of population in Maryland as well as in all of the other states, legislation is needed to provide an equalization fund so organized that all units may participate, and the State assume its fair share of the over-all costs of education in Maryland and in Baltimore City.

Under the legislation of April 29, 1949 additional aid from the State for the promotion of the building program was provided by the General Public Assistance Act of 1949. This Act [2] created a State debt of $20,000,000, the proceeds thereof to be used to supplement the financing of the construction of public school buildings in Baltimore City and the several counties. Apportionment was to be on the basis of enrollment up to a maximum amount equal to sixty dollars multiplied by the number of pupils enrolled, and at the rate of one dollar from the Assistance Loan for each three dollars spent by the county or the City of Baltimore for school building construction or sites. Total credit for Baltimore under the Act was set at $6,491,640.

Federal Assistance—The federal program for distributing government property declared surplus, with no cost to the recipient except for care and handling, continued to be an important source of comparatively new and hard-to-get equipment, thereby saving several hundred thousand dollars of the taxpayers' funds. Operating since June 30, 1949 under Public Law No. 152, 81st Congress, replacing Public Law 889, 80th Congress, hitherto in effect, the government distributed its surplus property through the

[2] Senate Bill 518, Chapter 502, Laws of Maryland 1949. Limited to five years from the date of passage.

State to tax-supported and tax-exempt schools, colleges, and universities with the Department of Education through its Supply Division acting as central distributing agent. Approximately sixteen trailer loads of materials were received each month throughout the biennium. Property for the Baltimore City schools was screened for school use by the supervisors of the various divisions.

Since 1943 the Department of Education has participated in the Federal Milk and Lunch Program whereby the Federal Government provides reimbursement for food purchases up to nine cents [3] for each Type A or "balanced"

TABLE 4
FEDERAL MILK AND LUNCH PROGRAM 1948-1950

Operation	1948-49	1949-50
Type A meals served to pupils in kindergarten, day-camp, nutrition, and orthopedic classes	62,765	58,953
Number of schools served	9	8
Meals sold	15,011	14,932
Meals served free of charge	47,754	44,021
Milk distributed (half-pints)	2,168,587	2,011,440
Number of schools served	107	106
Milk sold	1,427,459	1,346,203
Milk served free of charge	741,128	665,237
Reimbursement from Federal Government	$45,882.34	$23,630.42 [1]

[1] The smaller reimbursement this year reflects the reduction in government subsidy for Type A meals from 9 cents to 5 cents and in Type C meals (milk) from 2 cents to one cent.

meal served, and two cents for each half-pint of fresh whole milk. Under the terms of this arrangement, nearly $69,600 was contributed during the two-year period by the Federal Government through the State for food supplied free to the pupils in the schools and classes for anemic and physically handicapped pupils and to those attending the Highwood School. The statistical aspects of these operations are shown in Table 4. The same subsidy also applied to food served in the school cafeterias and served to reduce the cost of meals to the pupils.

[3] In 1949-50 reduced to five cents and one cent, respectively.

Increased Non-Resident Tuition Fees — A general increase of tuition fees amounting to approximately 20 per cent was authorized to take effect September 1, 1949. However, the Board did recognize special conditions which might warrant a reduction in rate in individual cases:

1. Any pupil who has been a resident of the City for one year or longer and is enrolled in the second semester of the final grade of any division of the school system when his parents cease to be residents of the City shall be treated as a resident pupil until the end of the semester in which the change of status occurs. This rule shall apply to pupils in 6A, 9A, 12A and the final grades or classes in the vocational education program.

2. Since the State aid which the City of Baltimore presently receives amounts to approximately $40.00 per pupil per year, a credit of that amount shall be granted to all residents of Maryland whose children are enrolled as tuition pupils in the Baltimore Public Schools.

3. In the case of Junior College students whose parents are not residents of Baltimore City but are taxpayers in the city, a tax credit may be allowed against that part of the operating cost which is provided through city funds. The amount of credit to be allowed in any case would be limited to the amount of the parent's total tax bill which is used for the support of the school.

4. Whenever a county pupil is domiciled in a city institution under the control of the Maryland State Department of Public Welfare a waiver of tuition will be authorized during the period of his commitment, provided that the enrollment of such pupil in a Baltimore public school has been requested by the superintendent of the institution and approved and recommended by the Superintendent of Public Instruction.

Benefits from the School Equipment Loan—In 1946-47, on the findings of a comprehensive survey of the furniture and equipment needs in all parts of the school system, it was conservatively estimated that over $4,500,000 would be needed to provide for the replacement of worn out and obsolete equipment and the purchase of additional items of equipment which would enable the teachers of Baltimore to carry on a modern instructional program with maximum efficiency. When the voters in 1947 and 1948 approved

TABLE 5

EXPENDITURES FROM EQUIPMENT LOAN FUNDS, JANUARY 1, 1948 THROUGH JUNE 30, 1950

Category	Fiscal Year 1948	Jan. 1, 1949 to June 30, 1950	Total Expended	Unencumbered Balance June 30, 1950
TOTAL EXPENDITURE	$1,027,820.90	$1,584,560.08	$2,612,380.98	$99,756.84
DEPARTMENTAL EQUIPMENT				
Art Education	22,618.59	28,346.50	50,965.00	57.71
Audio-Visual Education	14,891.50	55,549.48	70,440.98	2,365.02
Elementary Education	286,769.72	188,199.53	474,969.25	7,623.84
Music Education	36,921.32	104,914.62	141,835.94	774.31
... Education	44,917.38	95,459.65	140,377.03	1,435.91
School Library	52,433.49	81,722.72	134,156.21	21,161.03
Secondary Education [1]	115,348.85	113,760.06	229,108.91	11,683.78
Special ...	2,318.50	49,136.97	61,455.47	8,204.41
...al Education [2]	205,567.99	421,494.16	627,062.15	9,757.11
FURNITURE				
Elementary and Secondary	214,419.67	382,648.01	597,067.68	19,821.08
ADMINISTRATIVE OPERATIONS				
Janitorial and office	13,409.24	38,643.49	52,052.73	12,854.54
Reserve	8,204.65	24,684.89	32,889.54	4,018.10

[1] Does not include expenditures for industrial arts, home economics, business education, distributive education, occupational and shop centers, all of which are included in the vocational category.
[2] Includes expenditures for the subdepartments of the Vocational Division.

the Equipment Loans, totaling $3,000,000, they made possible a major step forward in the improvement of education in the Baltimore Public Schools. As a result every school received some new instructional equipment and classroom furniture to replace outmoded and outworn equipment. Recently developed equipment and audio-visual materials were added to facilitate learning in the industrial fields, the social studies, mathematics, science, and how to read, to write, to speak, to listen, and to think in a foreign language and in English. Opportunities .in art, music, and physical education were likewise extended in both elementary and secondary schools.

MODERN MANUAL AND ELECTRIC DUPLICATORS IN THE OFFICE PRACTICE LABORATORY STIMULATE BETTER LEARNING AND TRAINING FOR EMPLOYMENT

A more realistic approach in business, industrial arts, and vocational education was made possible through the purchase of modern equipment. More than half of the typewriters in use in the public schools in January, 1948, were over eighteen years old. Learning time was lost because of breakdown in equipment that was already beyond repair. Training in the use of modern office machines was not possible. With modern equipment in excellent operating condition students were motivated to develop skill in its use, to produce work acceptable according to actual business standards, and to learn how to give the care to this new equipment which employers have a right to expect of high-school graduates.

For years, especially during the war, there were practically no purchases of industrial arts equipment. The result was that tools became scarce and obsolete; and machines, even though kept in repair, were becoming too worn

LEARNING TO USE A LATHE IS AN IMPORTANT STEP IN UNDERSTANDING INDUSTRIAL PROCESSES AND IN TRAINING FOR EMPLOYMENT FOR BOYS WHO HAVE APTITUDE AND INTEREST IN THIS KIND OF WORK

out for efficient use. Many of the shops, especially at the two lower levels had no machines whatever, and only a small fraction of the hand tools needed for the classes which came to them. Through equipment loan funds, teachers were supplied with the tools and machines necessary to teach their courses without resort to improvised and inadequate substitutes for modern tools. In consequence the quality of the learning experiences of the pupils and their products have improved greatly. In the more advanced courses the acquisition of new precision instruments and new machines enabled teachers to provide realistic training on the level of modern industry.

Improvement of Buildings and Grounds

Although maintenance funds in the general operation budget for the fiscal years 1949 and 1950 were less than they were during the preceding two years, the schools continued to benefit from the loan appropriations of 1948 and the supplementary tax levy appropriation of 1950. A summary [4] of major improvements completed during the biennium is shown in Table 6.

The Coppin Teachers College

On September 15, 1949, the Board of School Commissioners adopted a resolution addressed to Governor William Preston Lane, Jr. requesting the Governor, as the executive head of the State of Maryland, to assume, as of September 1, 1950, the responsibility of providing for the education of colored teachers for Baltimore City and of transferring all or a part of the faculty of Coppin Teachers College to the State institution assigned the responsibility of training such teachers.

The resolution pointed out that the State of Maryland, since 1924, had assumed the responsibility for the training of white teachers because the city could not afford to undertake the building and development of an independent school for that purpose, and that the Board of School Commissioners planned to discontinue its operation of the Coppin Teachers College at the end of the 1949-50 school year because the Board did not feel justified in placing upon the city the tax burden required to make Coppin Teachers College a fully accredited institution. The transfer of Coppin Teachers College to the State was one of the

---

[4] For an itemized list of major improvements during 1946, 1947, 1948, 1949, and 1950 (to April) see *Superintendent's Newsletter*, vol. 3, 13-16, April 14, 1950

recommendations of the Maryland Commission on Higher Education, William L. Marbury, chairman, in its September 1, 1947 report. That the colored teachers of Baltimore, like those in the counties of Maryland, are entitled to a program of professional training in a fully accredited college seemed conclusive to the Board.

TABLE 6

SUMMARY OF MAJOR IMPROVEMENTS TO BUILDINGS

Operation	1948-1949		1949-1950	
	No. of Projects[1]	Amount Expended	No. of Projects[1]	Amount Expended
Buildings affected and total cost	72	$720,205	115	$867,437
Acoustical ceiling, new............	2	12,450	3	7,299
Ash hoist installation	1	1,960	—	—
Bitumuls paving	8	23,842	24	63,933
Building alterations	11	113,589	18	275,907
Electric wiring and fixtures....	10	129,625	12	106,236
Fence	1	1,513	1	1,091
Fire alarm systems, new..........	2	9,839	1	5,374
Flooring, new	9	21,727	5	11,881
Heating plant reconstruction..	9	92,677	6	44,416
Masonry pointing	—	—	1	14,800
Painting				
Interior	12	194,433	10	161,593
Exterior	3	66,207	6	77,754
Playground and athletic field				
equipment	3	15,780	5	16,063
Plumbing installation	4	9,090	7	35,192
Roofing, new	6	27,473	14	45,898

[1] Exclusive of jobs done by the Department of Education Repair Shop or any others which cost less than $1,000. For a detailed listing of these improvements see *Superintendent's Newsletter*, vol. 3, nos. 13-16, April 14, 1950, pp. 10 ff. Major work on buildings and grounds is covered by years, from August, 1946 to April, 1950.

The State of Maryland agreed to assume management of the Coppin Teachers College as of July 1, 1950, and assured the faculty of the college that their interests would be respected.

Teacher Recruitment and Training

The problem of teacher supply for the public schools is threefold: to secure candidates that are numerically suf-

ficient and academically qualified; to provide appropriate
training for beginning teachers; and to organize opportunities for professional growth for more mature teachers.
During the current biennium the first of these problems

TABLE 7

AVERAGE SIZE OF REGULAR CLASSES IN ELEMENTARY SCHOOLS AND
TEACHING SECTIONS IN JUNIOR AND SENIOR HIGH SCHOOLS

Year	Grades 1-6		Junior High		Senior High	
	White	Colored	White	Colored	White	Colored
1940	39.9	44.1	36.4	40.7	35.7	33.4
1941	40.8	43.4	36.3	36.1	33.7	28.6
1942	41.9	44.1	36.2	34.8	33.0	28.0
1943	42.6	43.6	36.5	34.5	35.0	27.8
1944	44.1	43.7	36.5	36.4	32.6	28.7
1945	41.2	42.5	35.0	38.6	32.4	28.9
1946	40.7	42.1	34.2	36.6	31.9	28.1
1947	40.6	41.2	33.9	35.6	31.6	37.6
1949	37.3	38.3	33.0	36.2	31.4	33.5

was especially acute by reason of the impending increase
in pupil enrollment resulting from the high birthrates of
the war years, which enhanced the need for elementary
teachers, and later for secondary teachers; and on account
of the troubled state of world affairs, the effect of which
was to deter young people, especially men, from preparing
for teaching as a career. To meet the turnover needs of
the white elementary schools there is required annually
a supply of not less than 230 new teachers; the colored
elementary schools require 100. In the white secondary
schools the number is close to 75, and in the colored secondary schools the number is about 50. These requirements also recognize the need for smaller classes, especially
in the elementary schools, if the findings of recent research
in child psychology are to be given effect in public schools.
The gratifying progress toward this end, which has been
attained despite rapidly increasing enrollments in recent

years and the necessity for part time in some schools, is shown in Table 7, which gives the average size of classes during the decade.

The actual number of teachers who entered service in the school year 1949-50 was 444, of whom 224 had never had any teaching experience, 98 were teachers who returned from leave of absence, 80 were from other states, 25 were from the Maryland counties, and 17 from private schools or colleges in Baltimore.

Internship Program—In addition to the new teachers who entered the system by successfully passing the professional examinations and the other concurrent requirements, a large group of promising young people who had graduated from liberal arts colleges without the education courses and the practice teaching which are required for admission to the Baltimore school system were accepted as special substitutes in the elementary schools and were given an opportunity to gain valuable experience under direction, preparatory to taking the professional examinations at a later date. Three different plans were developed. One plan involved an assistant relationship in which the intern worked with the head teacher in the classroom. Another plan released a head teacher from her classroom to guide the teaching activities of two, three, or four interns, each one of whom was assigned to a class of her own. The third plan placed an intern in a class under the guidance of the principal instead of a head teacher. During the two-year period 110 individuals participated in one of these three plans.

The intern observed the head teacher and learned how to study the children in her class. She attended demonstrations within and without her school building; participated in planning and evaluation conferences with the head teacher, principal, and grade supervisor; and shared experiences with other interns. She was introduced to professional books and periodicals and other opportunities for in-service training, including appropriate courses in curriculum areas and other fields which supplemented her practical experience and prepared directly for the professional examinations prerequisite for regular assignment.

The internship plan attracted young persons of desirable personal characteristics, good scholarship, and genuine interest in teaching. It enabled them to secure their needed professional preparation under desirable conditions of guidance. The length of internship varied from one week to one semester according to the background and maturity of the intern and to the type of plan being used. The schools that participated in the program obtained thereby better equipped special substitutes and opportunities for professional stimulation and growth.

Supervision—For the beginning teacher the supervisory program in the elementary school included demonstrations in the use of visual aids and field trips, assistance in dealing with some of the psychological problems of children, self-evaluation as to professional progress, and visitation with other probationary teachers who have common areas of interests.

More and more the concept of supervision for experienced teachers has centered on consultant and resource types of activities, largely through the staffs of supervisors in the offices of the several assistant superintendents. In addition to the many-sided services for the improvement of instruction which these people render, the workshops organized under the general direction of the Committee on Professional Development exemplify this trend. Especially noteworthy in this respect were the workshops on atomic energy and economics. The former provided opportunities for the members of the group to discuss with experts the scientific, military, political, industrial, and educational implications of nuclear fission. The workshop in economics presented authoritarian lectures and discussions on the national income, its total extent and the share of labor, the farmer, the business man, and the general consumer; monetary policy; savings and capital forma-

BEFORE THE EQUIPMENT LOAN 20,000 PUPILS SPENT EVERY DAY
IN OLD, UNCOMFORTABLE DESKS WHICH WERE DESIGNED 75 YEARS
AGO. TODAY'S MOVABLE FURNITURE MAKES POSSIBLE INTIMATE
GROUPS IN NORMAL LEARNING SITUATIONS

THE HOME ECONOMICS SUITE AT DOUGLASS HIGH HAS ALL MODERN
CONVENIENCES FOR LEARNING HOME-MAKING ARTS

tion; social security and social welfare; selling and buying in foreign markets; and improvement of economic understanding. Both of these workshops through their opportunities for audience-participation served to fortify teachers in their attempts to answer the questions of wide-awake youngsters in their classes. Another workshop, first organized in 1948-1949 and repeated in 1949-1950, grew out of an expressed desire on the part of a large group of teachers for help in the field of public relations. Basic concepts of good school-community relationships, community and advisory councils, open-house activities, conference with parents, student publications, community campaigns, Junior Red Cross, and Department of Recreation activities held in public schools were developed with the aid of authorities in special aspects of the problem.

In order to keep teacher-participation on a creative rather than a routine, perfunctory level the in-service program was based directly on the needs and interests of the staff as discovered through discussions in advisory committees and councils, in faculty and city-wide supervisory meetings, from informal conversations and interviews by central office personnel with individual teachers and principals, through contracts made by planning committees, and by direct request of the entire educational personnel through the *Superintendent's Newsletter.*

Committee on Professional Development

Workshops ranging in length from five to thirty hours, were also planned cooperatively by division heads, supervisors and their teachers. All requests were reviewed by the Committee on Professional Development, the central committee charged with the formulation and administration of opportunities for professional growth on the part of the supervisory and instructional personnel, so that they might be studied within the framework of system-wide needs and interests and in respect to the limitations of the budget allocated to professional study activities. In carrying out its mandate to provide a comprehensive program

HOOSING A CURRICULUM IS AN IMPORTANT MOMENT IN A STUDENT'S LIFE AND O
FOR WHICH THE COUNSELOR GATHERS COMPLETE INFORMATION PRIOR TO
INTERVIEWING THE STUDENT

of in-service opportunities for professional growth, the committee's catalog of workshops for 1948-49 listed a total of 59, of which 40 were new for that year. For 1949-50 the total listings numbered 62, of which 49 were new. There were also additional offerings in June and September of each year. This rich program was in addition to the wealth of education courses presented by the universities of the city.

Study Programs of Principals

Illustrative of the problems which concern the principals and vice-principals of elementary schools are the four enumerated below which comprised their study program for 1949-50.

1. Studying ways of helping beginning teachers

   Discussion groups made up of principals, vice-principals, and general supervisors and specialists in art, music, or physical education explored ways which the building leadership and the elementary supervisors were finding helpful in handling problems confronting teachers new to the system or just beginning their professional careers.

2. Gaining increased insight concerning the language arts program in the elementary school.

   Dr. Mary Alice Mitchell of Wilmington, Delaware, presented the concept of an integrated language arts program. Six observation-discussion groups were then organized to observe and evaluate language arts instruction in two primary and two intermediate grades.

3. Evaluating the effectiveness of new procedures for reporting pupil progress to parents

   New report cards developed by a city-wide committee of parents and school staff, based upon previous experimentation by seventy or more schools, were made available for optional use by schools. In May, 1950, an evaluation session was held in which the needed modifications and changes for another year were determined.

4. Studying the mental hygiene of staff relationships

   Problems of teacher-teacher relationships, teacher-principal relationships, the effect of administrative policies, the teacher who is seriously disturbed emotionally or is beginning to show signs of such disturbance, were studied with the aid of Dr. Alice V. Keliher of New York University as consultant.

Throughout the years 1948 and 1949 the principals of the secondary schools were encouraged to work in cooperation with their faculties on problems of particular significance to their individual schools and communities. In order to help them with their thinking a secondary school curriculum workshop was held in June, 1950, at which each school was represented by a team of not less than three, nor more than seven, faculty members. This number included the principal, vice-principal, and teachers who were appointed or elected to represent their faculty. When they came to the workshop these representatives brought with them the results of the thinking, reading, and studying on their individual problems for a year or more. At the workshop the big group was divided into sub-groups to work on the following common problems: meeting the needs of the slow learner; meeting the needs of the superior child; extracurricular activities; lay participation and the Community School; desirable relationships among the school staff; and following up of the school evaluation. Beginning in the fall, the schools studying in each of the above areas were to form councils so that as they built their new programs there would be a continued opportunity for an exchange of ideas. This plan gave each school the benefit of the thinking of all other participating schools and prevented an individual school from going too far in a direction which afterwards might prove to be unwise.

In the Division of Colored Schools principals of various schools held parent-teacher discussions on promotion policies and promoted the study of various ways of reporting to parents. They sponsored visits to reading clinics so that teachers might observe their organization and their remedial methods of instruction. They experimented with classes heterogeneously grouped, and the use of materials geared to various age levels. They also sought a better understanding of how to treat emotional problems exhibited by their pupils. They included visits to mental hospitals in their study program; and Dr. Arthur Lichtenstein and members of the Division of Special Services for Pupils, and Dr. Sybil Mandell, Chairman of the Public Education Committee of the Mental Hygiene Society, were invited to speak on various remedial methods that had been used successfully.

The curriculum became functional through the development of Friendship Gardens, Clean-Up Campaigns and Know Your Community units. A committee of laymen organized with administrative representation had the purpose of establishing an effective and constructive relationship between the schools and the community. Through visits to schools and educational centers, they developed an awareness of the scope of the educational program, its facilities and its needs.

Several principals initiated or continued experiments with integrated curriculum programs embodying various aspects of the so-called core curriculum. Garrison and Roland Park Junior High Schools continued their experimentation with homeroom-centered instruction in which the social studies and English were taught simultaneously and from common subject matter. Junior High School 106, Hill Street near Sharp, and Junior High School 137, Francis Street at Clifton Avenue, experimented along similar lines.

Parent-Teacher Organizations

Important contributions to the development and support of public education in Baltimore have been made by the 121 parent-teacher groups in the various schools. Such associations have been in existence in Baltimore for many years, each working independently. In October, 1947 these groups joined forces, organizing the Coordinating Council of the Baltimore Public School Parent-Teacher Organizations. Mr. Franklin O. Curtis was president of the council for two years, followed by Mr. R. Samuel Jett, who was elected in 1949.

This organization has been a very helpful instrument in promoting better educational opportunities for the children

PLAY AREA EQUIPMENT MAKES POSSIBLE HEALTH-BUILDING AND RECREATIONAL ACTIVITIES. SUCH OPPORTUNITIES ARE YET TO BE PROVIDED IN MANY BALTIMORE SCHOOLS

of the public schools of the city. It has been a means of spreading general lay understanding of the schools and their aims. It has studied school needs and made recommendations for the improvement of educational facilities. It has also been of great assistance in carrying the school loans.

In many other ways the council has given evidence of how valuable parents can be to the school system by their whole-hearted cooperation.

Personnel Policies

On February 5, 1948, a division of personnel was created in the Department of Education to administer the requirements of eligibility and selection prescribed in the Baltimore City Charter and the rules of the Board of School Commissioners; to formulate for the approval of the Board additional standards of qualification and eligibility for new positions and for other positions when needed; to act in an advisory capacity to the Superintendent and Assistant Superintendents in handling the individual problems arising with teachers already employed; to interview prospective teachers; to administer the credit provisions of the new salary schedule; and to recommend procedures by which groups of teachers whose training and experience were outside of the conventional pattern on which the single salary was predicated might benefit from the terms and provision of that schedule. This last-mentioned responsibility had an immediate and particular urgency, because on January 1, 1949, all educational personnel were to be on the new schedule, and there were many groups of faithful, efficient teachers who had met all of the requirements laid down in prior years, for whom special arrangements had to be devised lest their interests be unduly prejudiced by an unrealistic interpretation of the provisions of the new schedule.

In his study of these problems the director was aided by the Committee on Evaluation of Salary Credits, a standing

committee of directors, supervisors, principals, and teachers
nominated and elected by ballot by their co-workers to
review requests for salary increments requiring credits.
The function of the committee was to recommend to the
Board of Superintendents policies for the award of credit
toward advancement on the new salary scale in terms of
the broadened provisions previously approved by the Board
of School Commissioners,[5] and to evaluate submitted evidence of growth for salary credit. The first election was
held March 31, 1948. Half of the members retired at the
end of two years, the plan providing for the election of
new members to the committee every two years for terms
of four years each. The chairman of the committee was
to be appointed by the Board of Superintendents for an
indefinite term, and for this office the director of personnel
was selected.

Tentative policies were evolved by the committee with
regard to the conditions under which salary scale credit
should be granted for courses in art, dance, music, and
public speaking; and for work experience including camp
counseling, group and individual professional projects,
and participation in institutes and workshops outside of
those conducted by the Department of Education. The
deliberations of the committee were based on the premise
that the concept of professional growth should not be
limited to study at a college or university, but that growth
might very well result from service on important committees, the carrying out of significant studies or projects
in the classroom or on the playground, or the creation of
significant new or improved instructional materials or
methods. The committee members constantly review their
decisions, and past action is not necessarily considered
precedent. Frequent use is made of the help of consultants.

The Board of School Commissioners also approved a
number of far-reaching changes in personnel policies during the biennium. On January 20, 1949, it abolished the
long-standing policy of deducting a half-day's pay for each

---

[5] Enumerated in Report of the Board of School Commissioners, 1946-1948, page 35.

day a teacher was absent by reason of personal illness. These deductions had been made to provide a fund for the payment of substitutes. Under the new policy approved by the Board of School Commissioners, each educational employee is granted five working days' leave of absence

TABLE 8

ANNUAL SICK LEAVE ALLOWANCES FOR EDUCATIONAL EMPLOYEES, WITH ACCUMULATED MAXIMUM ALLOWANCE OF WORKING DAYS WITH FULL PAY AND HALF PAY AVAILABLE WITHIN THE CURRENT AND THE TWO IMMEDIATELY PRECEDING YEARS

Length of Service [1]	Annual Allowance Full Pay [2]	Maximum Allowance Three-Year Period (Days)
Less than 1 year......................	3 working days per mo.	30
1 year	5 working days	30
2 years	5 working days	40
3 years	5 working days	50
4 years	5 working days	65
5 to 9 years, inc......................	5 working days, ea.	95
10 to 14 years, inc..................	5 working days, ea.	130
15 to 19 years, inc..................	5 working days, ea.	150
20 to 24 years, inc..................	5 working days, ea.	170
25 years or more......................	5 working days, ea.	195

[1] Each *year of service* is to be interpreted as meaning up *to* but not *including* the next year of service.
[2] Schedule for four years and below effective January 5, 1950.

for personal illness each year and in addition the accumulated number of full-pay-allowance days which remained unused during the preceding years of his service in the Department of Education. Beyond this total he will also be entitled to leave with loss of half-pay up to a specified number of working days within a period of three consecutive school years. On January 5, 1950 the Board authorized a scale of graduated allowances for years of service up to five, since the previous actions of the Board did not provide for this graduation. With this revision the Baltimore sick leave policy stands as shown in Table 8.

A policy of sabbatical leave was approved by the Board of School Commissioners on March 16, 1950, to become effective July 1, 1950, the first time that such opportunity had been made available to Baltimore public school teachers. The principal provisions of the Baltimore policy follow:

1. The privilege of applying for sabbatical leave is open to all educational employees who have a record of satisfactory service of seven or more consecutive years.

2. The first leave for not more than one year may be granted after the seventh consecutive year of active service. The actual period of absence may be for one or two full semesters, as desired.

3. The purposes for which the leave may be granted are limited to study or travel or to such other activity as may be approved by the Board of School Commissioners on recommendation of the Board of Superintendents. Persons on sabbatical leave may not enter into gainful employment except upon the recommendation of the Superintendent and the approval of the Board of School Commissioners.

4. The status of the employee on leave is to continue as if he were on active service, and he is to be entitled to all the privileges thereof including pension benefits and contributions, credits toward salary increments, the right to promotion, and the assurance that he will not be transferred from his position unless he would have been transferred in the normal course of administrative operations.

5. The salary during the period of leave will be that to which the employee is normally entitled under the schedule *less* the minimum salary for a special substitute in the four-year training category; and, in the cases of persons receiving salary differentials, with the deduction of such additional sums as may be required to provide the necessary temporary replacements in the school system.

6. The method of selecting employees to be granted leave takes into consideration the number of qualified substitutes who are available for replacement purposes and limits the sum of all individuals on leave in any one year to a maximum of 3 per cent of all educational employees. This quota is to be distributed throughout the system so as to prevent any undue absence from any one school, from any single department within a school, or from any single division of the school system. From among all of those employees eligible for leave by virtue of

their service, those individuals who have served longest in the Baltimore Public Schools without receiving any sabbatical leave will be given first consideration.

7. Conditions imposed upon the recipient of sabbatical leave require that he shall agree to return to the service of the Baltimore Public Schools for at least one year following the expiration of his leave, or return to the City of Baltimore the salary which he received during the period of leave, *and* that he make such a report of his activities during the period of leave as may be requested by the Superintendent.

Eligible Lists—Two changes in the Rules regarding the eligible lists were made during the period. On May 5, 1949, the Board approved a recommendation that the section which provided that "no person shall be continued on any eligible list . . . for a period longer than one year and six months from the date of listing, provided the person has declined one or more assignments during this interval" be rescinded. The effect of this change will be to retain on the eligible list for a period of three years the names of all persons originally listed, whether or not they decline assignments which are offered them during that time.

The second change was made to clarify the order in which individuals whose names appeared upon eligible lists might be selected. The City Charter of 1898 had provided that nominations be made in the order in which names appeared. In the new Charter of 1946 it was merely stated that "the names of those qualified for appointment . . . shall be placed on the graded lists in the order of their relative qualification," with no commitment to the order of selection. At its meeting of May 18, 1950, the Board ruled that the Superintendent "limit his selection in the case of any particular vacancy to the five available persons standing highest on the appropriate list."

The Subversive Activities Act—From the date of the Governor's approval of the Subversive Activities Act of 1949, the so-called "Ober Law," the Department of Education has complied with Section 13 which requires public employees to file a written statement, under the penalties of perjury, that they are not personally engaged in acts or inciting acts intended to overthrow the Government by violence, nor members of organizations having this objective; and with Section 11 which imposes upon authorities which employ public employees, including teachers, the responsibility for determining that their applicants are

AMONG THE TOOLS MADE POSSIBLE BY THE EQUIPMENT LOAN WERE THOSE NEEDED BY TALENTED STUDENTS IN THE ART CURRICULUM

not engaged in treacherous activities by requiring them to file a written statement that they are not subversive and hence, under the 1949 amendment to the Constitution of Maryland, ineligible for public office. The Department of Education enforced these provisions throughout the current biennium while the Ober Act was under attack.

Baltimore Junior College

On February 2, 1947 an experimental upward extension of the public school system was inaugurated in the establishment of the Baltimore Junior College. From the beginning the college has been coeducational and under the direction of the assistant superintendent for secondary education. During the three and one-half years since its founding, it has become evident that there are at least four types of education that a public junior college in Baltimore should properly furnish:

1. The first and second years of work in the liberal arts and in pre-professional fields for those students who wish to transfer to higher educational institutions.

2. Technical programs in business and industrial training, including a core of general education, for those students who wish to terminate their formal education by preparing for employment at a pre-professional level.

3. General education for Baltimore students whose post-secondary education will be terminated in one or two years beyond graduation from high school.

4. Courses for adults whenever there is sufficient interest and demand to warrant the organization of classes.

Accordingly, courses were made available in the following areas in the scholastic year 1949-50: art, biology, business administration, chemistry, drafting, economics, electronics, English, history, languages (foreign), mathematics, merchandising, music, orientation, philosophy, physical education, physics, political science, psychology, recreational leadership, secretarial training, science survey, sociology, speech and dramatics, surveying, and technical training.

In addition, the college provides a full program of extra-curricular activities which it believes to be highly desirable in furthering its objectives. The program includes the student government organization, class-sponsored activities, a variety of clubs growing out of the curriculum, athletic and recreational opportunities in football, basketball (girls and men), baseball, lacrosse, track, fencing, swimming, rifle, gymnastics, tennis, archery, badminton, and golf for which the school provides equipment. These activities are supported in the main by the activity fee which is assessed against each student.

TABLE 9

PREPARATION OF JUNIOR COLLEGE GRADUATES ACCEPTED BY
HIGHER INSTITUTION

Area	Number
Total Graduates	41
Business, including business administration and accounting	10
Education	3
Engineering	2
Journalism	1
Law	6
Mathematics	2
Political economy	1
Pre-dental, -law, -medical	8
Psychology	3
Science, including biology and chemistry	5

To qualify for the degree of Associate in Arts at graduation, the student must have completed at least 60 semester hours with an average of "C" or better and have included in his curriculum English writing, English or American literature, natural science, social science, mathematics, physical and health education. In the semi-professional curricula at least 40 per cent of his work must be in courses applicable to his prospective vocation. To date 41 graduates have been accepted by institutions of higher learning: the University of Maryland 17; Western Maryland College 8; the Johns Hopkins University and the University of Baltimore 3; two each by George Washington, Gettysburg, and Loyola; and one each by the Baltimore College of Commerce, Bucknell University, University of Miami, and the Maryland State Teachers College.

Tuition fees per student were set originally at $300 per year for all students. Later this amount was reduced to

$150 per year for Baltimore City students, $250 for residents of Maryland outside of Baltimore City, and $350 for students who do not permanently reside in Maryland. These new fees resulted from the acceptance by city and state authorities of the principle that the State should bear one-third of the tuition cost of students who reside in Maryland, and the City one-third of the cost of students who reside in the City of Baltimore. In pursuit of that policy, the State appropriated $100 per student enrolled as a full-time matriculant. Beginning January 1, 1950, the city appropriated $50,000 for the support of the Baltimore Junior College. In addition to the tuition fee, laboratory fees (varying according to the type of course), graduation fees, and student activity fees are assessed.

Program for Children Having Cerebral Palsy

In accord with the national interest that has been developed in behalf of children suffering from cerebral palsy, the Baltimore Public Schools have long been interested in such children. For more than twenty years a changing group of from fifty to seventy cerebral palsy children have been successfully adjusted in the regular orthopedic classes, white and colored. In 1947, through a state plan authorized by the Children's Bureau of the Federal Government, a cooperative organization was set up involving the Maryland State Board of Health, the Baltimore City Board of Health, and the Baltimore Public Schools in order to serve better the needs of young children with cerebral palsy. Dr. Winthrop Phelps, a Baltimorean of international authority in the field of cerebral palsy, was the key person who acted as consultant and guide in planning for and medically counselling the new venture.

Two classes for white children of this type were organized at the William S. Baer School beginning September 1, 1947. One class was for fifteen five-year old kindergarten children; the other for fifteen primary-grade children of ages ranging from six to twelve. Ancillary to these classes

the following personnel, to be paid from state-federal funds,
were secured for medical and therapeutic services:

Number	Position	Time	Months
1	Medical Director	Part	10
1	Pediatrician	Part	10
1	Physical Therapist	Full	12
1	Occupational Therapist	Full	10
1	Speech Therapist	Full	10
2	Physical Therapist's Aides	Full	12
1	Stenographer	Part	12
1	Bus and Driver	Part	10

One class for fifteen colored children with cerebral palsy
was organized at the Francis M. Wood School beginning
September 1, 1948. The age range was from five to twelve.
The same number and type of medical and therapeutic
personnel as furnished the William S. Baer School were
provided the Francis M. Wood School from state-federal
funds. One teacher of academic subjects in each school was
furnished and paid by the Department of Education.

A typical day in the classes for these children begins
about 8:45 with the arrival of the buses. From the bus to
the classroom, some children are carried, some ride in wheel
chairs, and some are proudly able to walk in, alone. Each
has a locker for outer garments. After opening exercises
involving Bible reading, the oath of allegiance, and a song,
the formal work for the day begins. According to schedule
some children go to physical therapy for exercises, mas-
sage, and training in muscular coordination suitable for
walking or other motor activity. Others go to occupational
therapy for training in finer muscular adjustments, such
as dressing and undressing, feeding oneself, toiletry, and
the finger movements involved in pitifully slow, one- or
two-finger typing, or peg-clutched typing where a peg
replaces the finger. Sometimes the peg is even held between
the teeth. Other children go to speech therapy where a
trained clinician works through the various stages of the

long, slow process of teaching these children to talk. Practically all of the children need these three therapies.

In the kindergarten, the five-year olds, and a few older ones who have not yet reached a maturity level appropriate for academic work, are trained in group living, consideration for others, returning used objects to the places where they belong, finishing what is started, acquiring a selected oral vocabulary suitable for first grade work, and overcoming whimsical food habits in addition to the more conventional habits included in good kindergarten training.

In the primary room, approximately fifteen children are working in shifting groups on various stages of first, second, or third grade work. As they improve, both physically, through the three therapies, and academically, through the experiential teaching of the primary room, selected children are approved for promotion to the regular orthopedic classes of the school. This produces a normal flow of children to the main body of the school. To fill these places, promotion from kindergarten occurs, and so vacancies are provided for new five-year-olds each year.

Admission to the cerebral palsy classes and discharge therefrom is, as far as physical condition is concerned, upon the recommendation of the medical director. All children are received on trial, and if after the trial—typically two years—little or no improvement is noted, a committee representing all phases of the work considers the case, and, after deliberation, may request the parents to keep the child at home and provide for its future care and training in a private school or state hospital. Similarly children who endanger the safety of others and who chronically interfere with the instruction of others are either temporarily or permanently excluded. Approximately 85 per cent of the children are successfully adjusted.

In the regular orthopedic classes of the Baer School and of the Wood School are many more cerebral palsy cases than there are in the government-supported classes. These children continue to receive service from the therapists as advised by the medical director and proceed through the grades at approximately the same rate as other handicapped children. A few go through senior high school and college. Most cerebral palsy cases terminate their schooling somewhere in junior high school or in a vocational school or class. Those who graduate from junior or senior high are of course the better-endowed candidates. Several, indeed, have graduated from college and are making a successful adjustment in the Baltimore area at professional level. Vocational rehabilitation, however, is difficult for most cases. If they cannot hold a job in competitive industry, sheltered shop placement is indicated.

THE ENTIRE SCHOOL PROGRAM HAS BENEFITED BY THE IMPROVEMENT AND EXTENSION OF LIBRARY FACILITIES

Thus Baltimore has socially a program for children and youth who have been afflicted with cerebral palsy in which are integrated medical and therapeutic care, education, vocational rehabilitation and an opportunity for advancement as far as ability permits.

Administration of High School Athletic Program

Beginning with the fiscal year 1949 and continuing through 1950, an annual appropriation of $90,000 was included in the general budget of the Department of Education to cover the cost of the high school athletic program.

The advantages of this method of financing the athletic program on a fixed budget rather than having each school rely on gate receipts plus an allotment from a $15,000 revolving fund have been found to be far-reaching and sound:

1. The educational value of the program has attained new heights. It has ceased to be a commercial enterprise.

2. Inequities which existed among schools prior to 1949 were eliminated. A school with a losing football team is now assured of an adequate amount of money to finance the whole athletic program even though its gate receipts are lower than those of a school with a winning team.

3. Students and coaches are relieved of the "pressure to win" in order to collect enough money to carry on the total program of athletic activities.

4. Coaches in all schools are assured of full coaching salaries.

5. More activities can be provided to meet the needs, interests, and abilities of more students, and sufficient amounts are available for intramural athletics which offer opportunities for *all* students to participate in athletics.

6. The plan safeguards the student's health by reducing the frequency of contests and games, by making available better and safer equipment, by eliminating the necessity of playing games in inclement weather in order to collect gate receipts, and by engendering in staff physicians and coaches a new awareness of student health as the goal rather than its possible sacrifice for the winning of games.

7. Eligibility rules which were necessary under commercialized athletics can be eliminated. Under the new rule the principal is the judge of eligibility.

8. The plan eliminated the need for schools to play night football. Only three night games were played in 1950, whereas over twenty were played each year under the old system.

9. Competitive pressures were greatly reduced or eliminated: the pressure on schools to play "all-star" or exhibition games for large gate receipts; feelings of animosity among schools relative to securing the best "gate receipt" dates on the master football schedule; and the outside following which is interested in championships, standings of teams, star players, and gambling.

10. With gate charges in football and basketball reduced and charges in all other sports eliminated, more students are able to attend and enjoy games.

11. Excessive advertising of games is no longer necessary.

12. Under the new arrangement more officials are available to handle games.

MEMBERS OF THE MODERN PROBLEMS CLASS AT PATTERSON PARK SENIOR HIGH SCHOOL CONDUCT A
NEIGHBORHOOD SURVEY FOR THE DEPARTMENT OF RECREATION

The budgetary system of finance contributes to a recognition of athletics as an integral part of education. The athletic program is viewed as a laboratory for learning how to meet pressures similar to those in real life. Its direction should be under the guidance and control of school personnel trained and employed for that purpose. Coaches should be bona fide faculty members and, preferably, trained teachers of physical education. Coaching is teaching, and the primary concern of schools is education, not public entertainment or exploitation of boys for advertising or promotional purposes.

General Health Problems of Pupils

Distinct progress on several broad fronts was made during the biennium in meeting the health needs of pupils in the public schools. Through the funds provided by the Equipment Loan cots or beds were furnished for every health room where sufficient space was available; and an adequate supply of necessary small equipment—staplers, lenses, tweezers, screen curtains, first-aid kits, blankets, and bed linens—was procured on the basis of a per capita allotment of three cents per child in the elementary schools and four cents per pupil in other schools. Paper towels and soap were installed for the first time in *all* schools. In cooperation with the Baltimore City Health Department, the State Health Department, and the medical and dental profession a number of significant movements looking to the general betterment of the health of Baltimore children of school age were launched, and means were established for a better integration of all agencies concerned with the health of the school child.

Sodium Fluoride Treatments—On November 28, 1949, a sixteen-week program was inaugurated by a professionally trained team from the United States Public Health Service to provide dental fluoride treatment programs for elementary grade children in Schools 63, 83, 128, and 176. The purpose of this experiment was to demonstrate to parents, teachers, dentists, and public health authorities the use of an established technique for protecting the teeth of children. The Baltimore venture stemmed from a national program administered by the United States Public Health Service under an appropriation of one million dollars by the Congress in 1948.

The application to the teeth of the sodium fluoride solution is relatively pleasant; the two-per-cent aqueous solution is colorless, tasteless, and harmless if swallowed. It is applied directly to the dry surfaces of the cleaned teeth

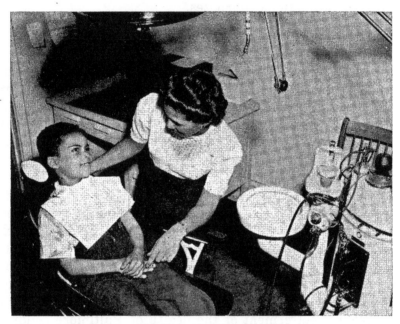

DENTAL CLINICS IN SCHOOLS CONTRIBUTE TO A WELL-ROUNDED
PRACTICAL PROGRAM OF HEALTH EDUCATION

and allowed to dry—a matter of about three minutes. This treatment is repeated every two or three days until the fluoride has been applied four times. Such treatment of school-age children at three-year intervals may be expected to give protection to all permanent teeth except the wisdom teeth, which ordinarily erupt in the late teens.

Each child who participated in the program was given a card to take home to his parents. The card described the treatment and advised the parents of the age at which the treatment should be repeated.

Maryland Dental Care Program—On February 27, 1950 the first dental clinic under the new Baltimore Dental Care Program opened in Canton Elementary School No. 230, Hudson Street and Highland Avenue. Shortly after, a second clinic was inaugurated in Elementary School No. 139, Central Avenue and Lexington Streets. Financed and administered by the Baltimore City Health Department, these clinics inaugurated a new program of dental care for school children as recommended by the committee of the Maryland State Planning Commission to study the medical care needs of Baltimore City. Dr. Lowell J. Reed of the Johns Hopkins School of Hygiene and Public Health was chairman of this committee. From its extensive studies of the dental care needs of Baltimore and other cities, the committee recommended that a dental care program be inaugurated in Baltimore that would have two branches: one, the treatment of the indigent and the medically indigent of the city; and the other, a constructive program for preventive care of the teeth of children in the public and parochial schools. In carrying out this program of prevention the committee concluded that it would be more effective to begin with the youngest age group and provide continuity of care to this group through future years in preference to providing limited services for a large number of individuals.

As a result of the recommendations by the above-mentioned committee, funds for the Dental Care Program were put into the budget of the City Health Department for the first time in 1949, and the program was inaugurated in February, 1950. The decision as to the schools to be used for the establishment of clinics was reached through conferences with the authorities representing the public and parochial school systems and the dental profession of Baltimore, with consideration given to the need for dental care, as indicated by relative socio-economic level, and to the limitations of the available funds. Additional clinics at School No. 6, Ann Street near Fleet, No. 55, Chestnut

Avenue and 37th Street, No. 76, Fort Avenue and Decatur Street, and No. 122, Preston Street near Pennsylvania Avenue, were planned for September, 1950.

During the first year of operation eligibility to participate in the program was limited to pupils who were unable to obtain dental service outside of the school, usually by reason of indigency, parental delinquency, or unwarranted hardship occasioned by the lack of dental facilities or their inconvenient location; and to children enrolled in the kindergarten and first grade. In the second year a similar program will be followed, but children then in the second grade will receive maintenance care. In this way the program will be extended to include children of an additional grade each year. Each clinic serves the public and parochial schools in its vicinity.

For its part in the support of the clinics, the Department of Education supplies such operating facilities as gas, electricity, and water, and ordinary room furnishings. The cost of salaries and the reconditioning of their dental equipment now in the schools is borne by the Health Department.

The program is expected to provide (1) an expansion of facilities and service, (2) emphasis on procedures designed to save teeth rather than to remove them, (3) routine annual inspection and follow-up of all children included in the program, (4) systematic inclusion in the program of children, beginning with the youngest age groups, making possible the greatest preventive effort, and (5) parent education. Only children who are otherwise unable to attain it will be given dental treatment.

The direction of the program is under Dr. H. Berton McCauley, first full-time director of the Bureau of Dental Care in the City Health Department.

School Health Council—On June 16, 1949 the Board of School Commissioners approved the establishment of the School Health Council, a joint undertaking with the Baltimore City Health Department, the Baltimore Council of

Social Agencies, and the medical and dental societies of the city, to coordinate the services of all the agencies interested in the health of Baltimore children. Under the plan of organization, the director of health and physical education of the Department of Education and the director of the Bureau of School Hygiene of the Health Department were designated co-chairmen. In addition to representatives of the other cooperating groups, the membership of the council embraced the assistant superintendents in charge of elementary, secondary, and colored schools, respectively, the director of kindergarten and primary grades, the supervisor of the health education, the supervisor of the school lunch program, two elementary and one secondary school principal, a representative from · the division of maintenance and operation, a school nurse, and three representatives of the Board of School Commissioners. The need for a coordinating organization of this type is especially urgent in Baltimore where health service in the elementary schools, public and private, is the responsibility of the city health department, and in the public secondary schools, that of the Department of Education.

The council considers problems in the major areas of health service for children, such as physical examinations and follow-up; health environment, including factors having to do with the maintenance and operation of building facilities; instructional program, including not only subject matter and activities in the field of health education but also such related aspects of the instructional program as eye strain and other physical strains, and the mental health concomitants. Many of the meetings of the council during this period were of an orientation type to acquaint the representatives with various aspects of the health program of the Department of Education and the Health Department. On June 19, 1950 the council conducted an open meeting to which all groups interested in school health were invited. Dr. Fred V. Hein of the American Medical Association and Dr. Allen O. Gruebbel of the American Dental Association served as consultants in a discussion of practical approaches to school health problems.

School Cafeteria Service—No more practical laboratory for the development of desirable health habits and nutritional values exists in any school than the school cafeteria or lunch room. This fact is becoming increasingly significant to the school system as the number of regularly organized and equipped lunch rooms in elementary schools steadily increases. During 1948-49 five new cafeterias were installed as well as one in each new building under construction. Elementary school lunch rooms serve only the Type A balanced lunch because young children need the food values of this type of midday meal even though they might not choose it for themselves. Junior high, senior high, and vocational schools in addition to featuring the Type A meal also have an a la carte service of soup, sandwiches, salads, desserts and ice cream. Under the terms of the Federal Milk and Lunch Program, which supplied government surplus foods and reimbursement for food purchases up to nine cents for each Type A meal served and two cents for each half-pint [0] of fresh whole milk, a Type A meal is defined as follows:

> A complete lunch providing one-third to one-half of the day's nutritive requirements and consisting of at least: (1) one half-pint of fresh whole milk as a beverage; (2) two ounces of meat or fish, or one egg, or two ounces of cheese; (3) one cup of vegetables or fruit, or one-half cup of each; (4) one or more slices of bread or muffins or other hot bread made of whole grain or enriched flour or cereal; (5) two teaspoons of butter or oleomargarine with added vitamin A.

From the Federal Government the schools received during the year cheese, fresh apples, butter, potatoes, canned corn, canned peaches, raisins, canned plums, turkey, fresh pears, honey, canned tomatoes, dried milk, peanut butter, tomato paste and dried eggs. When new shipments were received, menu suggestions and recipes were sent to the dietitians and managers to insure the best use of such commodities. Beginning in April, 1950 the Cafeteria Department was successful in securing a more nutritious bread through the cooperation of a local bakery and Dr. Clive McCay, Pro-

---

[0] In 1949-50 reduced to five cents and one cent respectively.

fessor of Nutrition, Cornell University, in whose laboratory the formula was developed. This bread combined improved flavor and texture with increased protein and calcium content through the addition of dry milk solids and soy flour.

Status of Cafeteria Department

On October 20, 1949, the Board of School Commissioners accepted the report of a committee of three Board members and three lay persons appointed by the President on April 7, 1949, to consider problems related to the operation of public school cafeterias, and approved its recommendations. These problems were concerned primarly with the relationship of the school cafeteria system to the other activities under School Board control and to the municipal government generally, the status of cafeteria employees, and the future administration of the cafeterias.

Instituted in 1922 with the organization of cafeterias at Clifton Park Junior High School and Forest Park High School, the administration of the system was delegated by the Board of School Commissioners to the Director of Vocational Education with the understanding that all expenses for operating the cafeterias, including the wages of personnel, expenditures for food, and other costs of operation, including the repair and replacement of equipment, would have to be paid out of cafeteria receipts. When new buildings were erected which included cafeterias, the original equipment was provided out of loan funds, but new cafeterias in existing buildings were financed entirely through cafeteria receipts and Federal subsidies. Every known precaution was taken to safeguard and account for the receipt and disbursement of cafeteria funds. Adequate records were kept and the books were audited annually by certified public accountants.

The committee recognized the efficiency with which the cafeteria system had been operated. Its chief concern was its exact legal status. It studied the provisions of the City Charter of 1946 which might have a bearing on this question. It reached the conclusion that the Charter requires the cafeteria system to be operated according to an annual budget provided for in the Ordinance of Estimates; that cafeteria personnel be employed under the same conditions as all other employees of the School Board; and that the administrative procedures be similar to those followed in the school system generally, with all future receipts and disbursements handled and accounted for as municipal funds.

On the basis of these findings and its study of cafeteria personnel the committee submitted a number of recommendations, most of which, through conference with the city authorities and legislation where needed, were being made effective by the end of the school year. Those enumerated below indicate the major policies that were proposed.

1. That beginning January 1, 1950, the public school cafeterias be operated as an administrative division of the public school system in accord with the general policies which govern all other school functions.

2. That the responsibility and authority for the cafeteria program be assigned by the Superintendent to an assistant superintendent to whom the supervisory and other personnel in cafeterias will be responsible.

3. That the budget for school cafeterias be included annually in the Ordinance of Estimates, as a self-supporting section, beginning January 1, 1950.

4. That dietitians and supervisory personnel be employed in the same manner as other educational personnel.

5. That all cafeteria employees below the grade of dietitian be included in the Classified Service and treated in full accordance with the legal provisions governing other classified employees in the employ of the Board of School Commissioners.

6. That all cafeteria employees be offered, as soon as possible, membership in the Employees' Retirement System of Baltimore City, with credit for service prior to the date of their entry into the system.

7. That agreement be sought with the city authorities to retain reserve funds in cafeteria accounts for cafeteria purposes, such as the installation of new cafeterias in existing buildings and the renovation of obsolete equipment.

Under new legislation the full benefits enjoyed by other employees of the Board of School Commissioners were provided for the employees of the Cafeteria Department. Because of the educational nature of their work and its close relation to the instructional programs of the schools, dietitians who are employed in accord with standards of professional education similar to those required of teachers are to be considered educational employees and paid on a salary scale similar to that of teachers. Thus a continuance of the highly efficient service of the Cafeteria Department was assured without setback.

II

THE CAPITAL IMPROVEMENT PROGRAM

Continuous progress on many fronts, despite unavoidable and irritating delays, marked the evolution of the Capital Improvement Program during the biennium. Approaching completion for occupancy in September, 1950, were the major addition to the Benjamin Franklin Elementary-Junior High School, Cambria and Twelfth Streets, Curtis Bay, and the gymnasium and shops building at the Dunbar Senior-Junior High School, Caroline and Jefferson Streets. The new Fallstaff Road School was expected to be ready for pupils in January, 1951, and the new Graceland Park-O'Donnell Heights School, O'Donnell and Gusryan Streets, in February, 1951. Also under contract and in process of construction was the Fannie L. Barbour Elementary School at Saratoga and Schroeder Streets for colored pupils. On the drawing boards but well into final stages of approval were the building for the combined Edison-Barton-Mergenthaler vocational high school at Hillen Road and 35th Street, an additional floor for School No. 139, Central Avenue and Lexington Street, the Cherry Hill Elementary School, Cherry Hill Road and Seabury Avenue, the Armistead Gardens Elementary School and the Northwood Elementary School. At this stage also were major additions to the Booker T. Washington Junior High School at Madison and Lanvale Streets, School No. 18, Druid Park Drive, and No. 88, Wildwood Parkway. Preliminary drawings and studies were being made for the elementary school at Mt. Winans, the Southwest Baltimore Colored Elementary School at Barre and Warner Streets, the junior high school at Cherry Hill, the gymnasium building for School No. 106, Hill Street near Sharp, and the Carver Vocational High School at Presstman and Bentalou Streets, so long delayed by difficulties of site procurement.

The program of advance site acquisition moved steadily forward in all sections of the city. Each site recommended by the Board of School Commissioners must be approved

TABLE 10

Sites for Future Buildings Acquired under Fifth and Sixth School Loans

Code Number [1]	Name and Location	Acreage	Status of Site June 30, 1950	Amount Paid to June 30, 1950
71D-11	Edison-Barton-Mergenthaler Vocational High School No. 410, Hillen Road and 35th Street	17.0	Acquired by purchase 1946	$156,365.57
71D-12	Southwest Baltimore Elementary School No. 162, Barre, Lee, Warner, and Greene Sts.	2.25	Acquired by purchase April 17, 1949	229,457.93
71D-16	North Baltimore Junior High School, Woodbourne and Beauregard Avenues	13.3	Acquired by purchase May 16, 1947	70,558.64
71D-19	Northern Parkway Elementary School, Gleneagle Road and Leith Walk	7.36	Acquired by purchase October 26, 1947	42,556.42
71D-24	Cross Country Boulevard Elementary School, Cross Country Blvd. and Taney Road	4.2	Acquired by purchase May 7, 1948	25,614.55
71D-30	Addition to Harvey Johnson Junior High School No. 106, Hill Street near Sharp	.74	Acquired by purchase March 18, 1949	12,892.50
71D-31	Northwood Elementary School No. 242, Loch Raven Boulevard and Hartsdale Road	14.5	Acquired by purchase October 28, 1948	80,236.50
71D-32	New site for Carver Vocational High School No. 454, Presstman and Bentalou Streets	13.5	Acquired by purchase February 4, 1949	49,398.13
71D-33	Armistead Gardens Elementary School No. 243, Erdman Avenue and Eager Street	7.55	Acquired by purchase October 29, 1948	1,137.66 [2]
71D-34	Carter G. Woodson Elementary School No. 160, Cherry Hill and Seabury Roads	11.86	Acquired by transfer from Health Department, January 26, 1949	7,106.97
71D-36	Additional site for Southern High School No. 70, Warren Avenue and William Street	....	In process of acquisition	....
71D-40	West-Southwest Senior High School, Edmondson and N. Athol Avenues	26.04	Acquired by purchase March 13, 1950	135,086.60

[1] School Loan Allotment Number

TABLE 10 (Continued)

SITES FOR FUTURE BUILDINGS ACQUIRED UNDER FIFTH AND SIXTH SCHOOL LOANS

Code Number [1]	Name and Location	Acreage	Status of Site June 30, 1950	Amount Paid to June 30, 1950
71D-43	New site for Mount Winans Elementary School No. 156, Huron and Harman Avenues	3.37	In process of acquisition	$ ....
71D-44	Cherry Hill Junior High School No. 360, Cherry Hill Road and Seamon Ave.	9.56	Acquired by purchase December 16, 1948	32,506.20
71D-46	Bay A.. ue Elementary School, Callaway, Fernhill and Lewin Av nues	4.14	Acquired by purchase May 11, 1950	55,444.28
71D-47	Gwynns Falls Parkway Elementary School, Gwynns Falls Parkway and Dukeland Street	9.18	In process of acquisition	....
71D-48	Bragg School for Boys, E.. ..in Av nu Extended	32.0	In process of acquisition	2,524.50
71D-49	Additional site for the Highwood School, No. 300, Maiden Choice Lane	1.1	In process of acquisition	....
71D-50	Frederick Road Elementary School, Frederick Road and Martingale Ave.	7.5	In process of acquisition	....
71D-52	Edgecombe Circle Elementary School, Edgecombe Circle and Virginia Ave.	8.75	Acquired by purchase February 14, 1950	33,129.13
71D-53	For School No. 107, Pennsylvania R.R. surface rights near Laurens Street from Whatcoat to Gilmor Street	.95		
	For School No. 112A, Pennsylvaniaa R.R. surface rights near Laurens Street betn ..at and Calhoun, and Cal hun and ..ar Streets	.33	Acquired by purchase February 2, 1950	22,756.00

TABLE 10—Continued

SITES FOR FUTURE BUILDINGS ACQUIRED UNDER FIFTH AND SIXTH SCHOOL LOANS

Code Number [1]	Name and Location	Acreage	Status of Site June 30, 1950	Amount Paid to June 30, 1950
71D-54	Medfield Heights Elementary School, Roland Heights and Buchanan Avenues	3.5	In process of acquisition	$21,958.93
71D-55	Frankford Avenue Elementary School, Frankford Avenue and Susquehanna Transmission Line	11.39	Acquired by purchase November 10, 1949	18,857.83
71D-57	Addition to Gardenville Elementary School No. 211, Belair Road and Frankford Avenue	.57	Acquired by purchase January 10, 1950	14,102.60
71D-58	New site for Lauraville Elementary School No. 155, Craddock and Linworth Avenues	4.7	In process of acquisition	....
71D-59	East Bal the Colored Elementary School, Washington, Chase and Wolfe Streets	2.25	In process of acquisition	12,928.67
71D-62	Brooklyn-Curtis Bay Elementary School, West Bay ... and H ner Court	7.4	In process of acquisition	....
71D-63	Brooklyn Hills High School, Sixth Street opposite Deck ...	....	Pending approval of the Department of Planning	....
71D-66	Lakeland-Dorchester Heights Elementary School, Hollins Ferry Road and Wedgeworth Lane		Pending approval of the Department of Planning	....
71D-67	McLean Boulevard Elementary School, McLean Boulevard and Pinewood Avenue	8.38	In process of acquisition	....
71D-68	East Baltimore Junior High School, Sinclair and Bowley's Lanes	22.7	In process of acquisition	....

[1] School Loan Allotment Number.

by the Municipal Department of Planning before its acquisition by the Real Estate Agency of the Mayor and City
Council can be authorized. Procurement of sites in advance
of population movements and before the erection of improvements thereon not only insures a great saving in
cost to the taxpayers but eliminates delay when the time
comes for a building to be erected. Because suitable sites
for needed buildings in congested areas were not available
from previous building programs, the current program was
greatly hindered in its early years.

Scope of the Building and Site Program

The Capital Improvement Program thus far recommended by the School Plant Planning Committee and approved by the Board of School Commissioners embraced
five different types of enterprises: (1) the completion of
projects deferred from previous programs: the Forest
Park swimming pool and the erection of new plants for
vocational education; (2) the acquisition of available buildings that could be adapted to meet specific needs: the
Bragg Home, Old Frederick Road, to be used for a "High-
wood" program for colored youth; four buildings to extend
the facilities for vocational education; 2418 St. Paul Street
to supplement the facilities of the Administration Building
at 3 East 25th Street and to improve the automobile park-
ing situation; a storage building at Light and Heath
Streets; and two elementary school plants purchased from
the Federal Government: Elementary School No. 238,
Chesapeake Avenue and Sun Street, and a temporary classroom building of five rooms, including equipment, located
on rented land at Holabird and Bob White Avenues; (3)
the design and construction of major additions and new
buildings; (4) the development of play areas and physical
education facilities; and (5) site purchases for future
buildings. Tables 10 to 15 give detailed information regarding the building and site projects in these five groups. Together they comprise the entire list of projects which the
Board of School Commissioners had reasonable expecta-
tions of completing from the funds made available through

No.	Building	Location	Cost		Date
153	Elementary School 71D-28b	Holabird and Bob White Avenues	$ 700 [2]	$	Aug. 12, 1949
153A	Elementary School 71D-28a	Holabird Avenue and Broening Highway	61,236 [3]	......	1948
238	Victory Elementary School 71D-29	Chesapeake Avenue and Sun Street	13,820 [4]	......	Aug. 12, 1949
451	Joseph C. Briscoe General Vocational School 71D-17	Druid Hill and Lafayette Avenues	55,000 [5]	2,238	April 30, 1947
452	General Vocational School 71D-41	Biddle and McCulloh Streets	229,268	97,036	Dec. 14, 1948
503x	Warehouse 71D-26	Light and Heath Streets	117,896	......	Aug. 2, 1948
522	Administration Building Addition 71D-42	2418 St. Paul Street	46,111	5,303	Dec. 7, 1948

[1] In addition to the buildings listed in this table, buildings at the following locations were acquired during the period 1947-1950 through federal veterans' ... funds; Loch Raven Road and Fillmore Street, 585 West Preston Street, 2614 Pennsylvania ... ue.
[2] Prefabricated structure. Title acquired from Federal Government.
[3] Prefabricated structure ... on land ... by Housing Authority of Baltimore City. Buildings purchased from manufacturer and erected on site by Department of Education.
[4] Purchased from Federal Government. The transaction included two s..., for which a consideration of $200 was paid.
[5] Includes property at 415 Lafayette Avenue, ... of Druid Hill ...ue.

TABLE 12

Buildings Being Constructed under Fifth and Sixth School Loans June 30, 1950

School No.	Name of School	Location and Acreage	Facilities [1]	Architect	Cost of Site	Amount and Date of Contract
133	Dunbar Junior-Senior High School Addition 71D-25	McElderry and Caroline Streets	1 classroom, 12 shops, gymnasium	Gaudreau & Gaudreau	$ .... [2]	$ 943,830 Apr. 20 1949
161	Fannie L. Barbour Elementary School 71D-8	Saratoga and Schroeder Streets 2.65 acres	24 classrooms, general-purpose room, gymnasium, auditorium, library, 2 kindergarten rooms, cafeteria, health suite	Francis J. Han	300,679	1,023,450 Jan. 11 1950
239	Benjamin Franklin Junior High School Addition 71D-27	Cambria and Fifth Streets Brooklyn	11 classrooms, general-purpose room, cafeteria, auditorium, 2 shops, library, health suite, gymnasium	Zink & Moehle	.... [2]	1,088,000 May 11 1949
240	Graceland Park-O'Donnell Heights Elementary School 71D-18	Dell and Gusryan Streets 10.44 acres	21 classrooms, cafeteria, auditorium, health suite, library, 2 kindergarten rooms, gymnasium	Hall, Border, & Donaldson	70,729	1,060,935 Nov. 30 1949
241	Fallstaff Road Elementary School 71D-10	Fallstaff Road and Gist Avenue 4.33 a res	12 classrooms, cafeteria, auditorium, gymnasium, health suite, library, general-purpose room, kindergarten room	Wrenn, Lewis & Jencks	23,668	504,750 Aug. 20 1948

[1] In each case the building of a gymnasium includes also showers and lockers.
[2] Built on existing site.

TABLE 13

PHYSICAL EDUCATION FACILITIES ACQUIRED UNDER FIFTH AND SIXTH SCHOOL LOANS UP TO JUNE 30, 1950

Name of Project	Location	SITE DATA		Cost to June 30, 1950	Other Cost to June 30, 1950	Total Cost to June 30, 1950
		Acreage	Date			
Playground, School No. 2 71D-56	Stiles and Lloyd Streets	0.5	December, 1949	$30,000 [1]	$	$ 30,000
Playground, School No. 70 71D-13	Warren Avenue and William Street	0.78	January, 1947	32,345	7,890	40,235
Playground, School No. 85 71D-9	Lakewood Avenue and Oliver Street	3.38	December, 1945	21,758 [1]	25,568	47,326
Playground, School No. 220 71D-15	Washington Boulevard and Spence Street	0.3	December, 1946	11,485	......	11,485
Playground, School No. 298 71D-7	North Avenue and Broadway	2.135	June, 1945	42,916	26,882	69,798
Swimming Pool, School No. 406 71D-64	Chatham Road and Eldorado Avenue	......	......[2]	107	......	......
Athletic Field, Clifton Park 71D-38	Area No. 5, Clifton Park	......	June, 1950	393 [1]	677	1,070
Athletic Field, Kirk Avenue 71D-23	Kirk and Exeter Hall Avenues	11.75	November, 1940	98,667	160,649	259,316
Athletic Field, Patterson Park 71D-37	Patterson Park	......	......	......[1]	......	......

[1] Joint project with Department of Parks and Recreation. Amount shown is Department of Education's share of site cost.
[2] Space for pool excavated when building was originally constructed, 1924. At this writing $107 has been spent; the contract price being $42,488.

ELEMENTARY SCHOOL NO. 241, FALLSTAFF ROAD AND GIST AVENUE

ELEMENTARY SCHOOL NO. 161, SARATOGA AND SCHROEDER STREETS

ADDITION TO JUNIOR HIGH SCHOOL NO. 239, CAMBRIA AND TWELFTH STREETS

TABLE 14

BUILDINGS IN THE PLANNING STAGE JUNE 30, 1950

School No.	Name of School	Location	Facilities	Architect
18	Franklin D. Roosevelt Elementary School Addition 71D-39	Druid Park Drive between Liberty Heights Avenue and Reisterstown Road	6 classrooms, auditorium-gymnasium, library	David Harrison
70	Southern Junior-Senior High School Addition 71D-36	Warren Avenue and William Street	17 classrooms, shop, library, swimming pool, gymnasium, bath suite	Henry Powell Hopkins
88	Lyndhurst Elementary School Addition 71D-45	Wildwood Parkway near Edmondson Avenue	8 classrooms, general-purpose room, library	Benjamin Frank
106	Harvey Johnson Junior High School Addition 71D-30	Hill Street near Sharp	Gymnasium	Ewald
130	Booker T. Washington Junior High School Addition 71D-35	Lafayette Avenue and McCulloh Street	14 classrooms, 2 gymnasiums, 6 shops, auditorium	Tyler, Ketcham, & Myers
139	Elementary School Addition 71D-61	Central Avenue near Lexington Street	7 classrooms	Buckler, Fenhagen, Myers & Ayers
156	Mount Winans Elementary School 71D-43	Huron and Harmon Avenues	9 classrooms, general-purpose room, health suite, library	William Gray
160	Carter G. Woodson Elementary School	Cherry Hill Road and Seabury Avenue	20 classrooms, cafeteria, library, gymnasium, auditorium	Adams & Rigg

BUILDINGS IN THE PLANNING STAGE JUNE 30, 1950

School No.	Name of School	Location	Facilities	Architect
162	Southwest Baltimore Elementary School 71D-12	Barre, Warner, Greene, and Lee Streets	23 classrooms, auditorium, library, gymnasium, cafeteria, general-purpose room, 2 kindergarten rooms, clth suite	John A. Ahlers
242	Northwood Elementary School 71D-31	Loch Raven Boulevard and Hartsdale Road	23 classrooms, general-purpose room, 2 kindergarten rooms, auditorium, library, gymnasium, cafeteria, health suite	Jamison & Marcks
243	Armistead Gardens Elementary School 71D-33	Erdman Avenue and Eager Street	21 classrooms, auditorium, 2 kindergarten rooms, gymnasium, library, cafteria, community room, health suite	Finney, Wolcott, & Associates
360	Cherry Hill Junior High School 71D-44	Cherry Hill Road and Seamon Avenue	33 classrooms, auditorium, library, gymnasium, 3 shops, health suite, cafeteria	Gaudreau & Gaudreau
410	Edison-Barton-Mergenthaler Vocational High School 71D-11	Hillen Road and West 35th Street	40 classrooms, 60 shops, 2 libraries, swimming pool, gymnasium, prekindergarten room, auditorium, cafeteria, health suite	Taylor & Fisher
454	Carver Vocational High School 71D-32	Bentalou and Presstman Streets	16 classrooms, 37 shops, gymnasium, swimming pool, library, health suite, cafeteria, auditorium	William E. Stone, Jr.

TABLE 15
FUTURE PROJECTS FOR WHICH LOAN FUNDS WILL BE REQUIRED
(Construction Priority Not Determined to Date)

Project	Estimated Cost
Total Estimated Cost	$70,125,000
Addition to Administration Building	1,170,000
Addition to No. 132, Mount and Mulberry Streets	600,000
Addition to Warehouse and Shops	650,000
Additional athletic fields and stadiums	250,000
Additional portables	200,000
Additional sites	100,000
Additions to existing sites	5,000,000
Brooklyn Hills Senior High School	1,700,000
Callaway Avenue Elementary School	565,000
Cross Country Boulevard Elementary School	1,070,000
Curtis Bay Elementary School	1,070,000
East Baltimore Senior High School	4,300,000
Edgecombe Circle Elementary School	1,095,000
Frankford Avenue Elementary School	1,095,000
General vocational schools	4,800,000
Gwynns Falls Parkway Elementary School	1,590,000
Improvements to existing facilities	10,000,000
Junior college	2,800,000
Lakeland-Dorchester Heights Elementary School	470,000
Leith Walk Elementary School	1,035,000
McLean Boulevard and Pinewood Elementary School	1,120,000
Medfield Heights Elementary School	580,000
North Baltimore Junior High School	2,500,000
N.W. Baltimore Colored Elementary School	1,900,000
N.W. Baltimore Colored Junior High School	3,000,000
N.W. Baltimore White Junior High School	2,900,000
Pimlico Road near Western Run Elementary School	1,170,000
Relief for No. 71, Old Frederick Road	1,170,000
Relief for No. 211, Belair Road	1,120,000
Replacement for No. 14, Linden Avenue	1,180,000
Replacement for No. 118, Argyle Avenue	1,420,000
Replacement for No. 115, Merryman's Lane	560,000
Replacement for No. 155, Beauregard Avenue	460,000
Replacement for No. 154, Fairfield Road	480,000
Replacement for No. 114, Caroline Street	1,180,000
Replacement for No. 33 and No. 92, South Baltimore	1,850,000
Replacement for No. 23, Wolfe Street	980,000
Sinclair Lane Elementary School	1,145,000
Sinclair Lane and Moravia Junior High School	2,600,000
Western High School, Athol and Edmondson Avenues	3,250,000

the Sixth School Loan augmented by a $9,000,000 balance unexpended from the Fifth School Loan and $6,491,640 received from the State of Maryland under the terms of the General Public Assistance Act of 1949 to aid the counties and thé city in the construction of public school buildings.

However, the studies of the School Plant Planning Committee and the School Board have indicated clearly that the needs of the system for new construction far exceed the number of facilities already approved. Table 15 indicates projects which these groups have already agreed should be undertaken as soon as funds become available. In addition to the specific projects listed therein there are the many obsolete buildings and playgrounds scattered throughout the city which will be in service a long time and should be modernized to enable them to provide a well-rounded program for their children. Most of these plants were cited by the Strayer Survey for replacement or rehabilitation. Some of the structures were erected more recently but still are without facilities deemed essential under present standards. Thus the building problems of Baltimore cannot be solved by intermittent school loans every few years, but they must be thought of as a continuing program of providing modern facilities for oncoming school populations.

Determination of Building Needs

From 1920 the over-all growth of full-time day schools climbed steadily to a peak of 119,692 in 1935, after which the effects of the depression-reduced birth rates brought the number of students down to a low point of 105,135 in 1945. Since that year there has been a marked upswing in the number of births, and already the number of pupils to be housed has reached a total of over 118,000 pupils. And the number is expected to mount much higher, as Table 16 indicates. But while this pattern of growth was prevailing in the schools as a whole, the trend in the white and colored schools, respectively, was somewhat different. The white

TABLE 16

ELEMENTARY SCHOOL ENROLLMENT AND BIRTHS SIX YEARS EARLIER,
WITH ESTIMATED ENROLLMENT TO 1962

| Oct. 31 Year | WHITE SCHOOLS | | | COLORED SCHOOLS | | |
	Elementary Net Roll	Births [1] Six Years Earlier	Birth Rate	Elementary Net Roll	Births [1] Six Years Earlier	Birth Rate
1935	58,853	10,851	16.5	22,271	3,138	22.4
1936	56,903	10,731	16.2	22,589	3,141	21.9
1937	55,031	10,130	15.2	23,145	3,032	20.8
1938	53,310	9,737	14.6	23,382	3,048	20.6
1939	50,986	9,130	13.6	23,553	3,059	20.4
1940	49,470	9,196	13.6	24,018	3,005	19.7
1941	48,820	9,363	13.8	24,184	2,969	19.2
1942	49,496	8,956	13.1	24,359	2,845	18.1
1943	50,091	9,370	13.7	24,535	3,146	19.7
1944	48,337	9,892	14.4	25,225	3,316	20.4
1945	46,207	9,211	13.3	25,585	3,314	20.1
1946	45,827	10,105	14.6	26,048	3,607	21.6
1947	46,638	11,886	17.0	26,978	4,109	24.4
1948	48,603	15,076	20.1	28,109	4,644	25.6
1949	49,530	16,077	21.0	29,463	4,977	25.0
1950	50,790 [2]	14 021	18.5	30,297 [2]	4,809	26.6
1951	51,905	13 308	17.8	31,223	4,540	24.9
1952	54,720	15,805	21.1	32,643	5,306	29.1
1953	57,554	17,799	23.6	34,430	6,193	31.9
1954	58,227	15,414	20.4	36,068	6,669	33.2
1955	59,850	14,335 [3]	18.9	37,711	7,080 [3]	35.0
1956	60,713	12,623	16.5	38,775	6,450	30.0
1957	61,157	12,020	15.6	39,450	5,873	27.0
1958	59,685	11,873	15.3	39,653	5,500	25.0
1959	56,988	11,801	15.1	38,525	5,118	23.0
1960	55,843	11,805	15.0	36,247	4,500	20.0
1961	54,727	11,887	15.0	33,591	4,550	20.0
1962	54,231	11,970	15.0	31,648	4,600	20.0

[1] Resident births supplied by the Baltimore Department of Health.
[2] Estimates supplied by Department of Health are given in italics and are subject to revision in later years.
[3] The data for 1955 referring to birth year 1949 are provisional; the birth data that follow are estimates. These figures form the basis for estimating the elementary net roll from 1955 to 1962.

schools reached their peak in 1932 and thereafter declined rapidly and steadily to a minimum in 1946. In the colored schools, however, the decline in births was offset by continuous in-migration during the depression sufficient to maintain a steady increase in enrollment up to 1940. During the next three years, 1941 to 1943, enrollment remained practically stationary, pending a further resumption of its upward climb in 1944. That these upward trends will continue at rapidly accelerating rate is indicated by the steady rise in births during the war years and afterwards.

These estimates, which were computed for the Bureau of Measurements, Research, and Statistics by Dr. W. Thurber Fales of the Baltimore City Health Department, were derived from the number of resident births in the city each year, the operation of factors affecting total city population such as in-migration and out-migration, and the relative distribution of pupils within the school system. As new data become available annually, the processes and the assumptions are revised so that a high degree of accuracy is obtained. The error of prediction for 1948 was 3.1 per cent; the following year it was reduced to one half of one per cent. Even though differences between actual enrollments and estimates may prove to be greater in subsequent years, it is certain that future increases in net roll will be very great.

Although it is evident that for the city as a whole an increased enrollment of pupils in the immediate future is in prospect, the problem of housing these pupils has been greatly complicated by large-scale movements of population within the city. In hitherto undeveloped areas sites were secured as rapidly as possible at locations so situated with respect to each other that no child would be required to travel more than one-half mile to reach elementary school or one mile to reach a junior high school, and in accordance with the Master School Plan which was developed in the Division of School Facilities so as to provide complete coverage of the city with respect to new school construction.

To aid the School Plant Planning Committee in its study of specific sections of the city where new school construction appeared to be needed, as many indexes of future school population were assembled as could be obtained from the data in the Department of Education and through the generous cooperation of the Health Department, the Department of Planning, the Housing Authority of Baltimore City, the Baltimore Redevelopment Commission, and the Bureau of Plans and Surveys. These indexes included trends in school enrollment over a period of years, trends in births in the study area, the ratio of school enrollment to births, the number of housing units for which construction had been approved and/or permits issued, the number of children per unit in existing housing, (especially where large-scale private and public housing is involved), plans for new public housing or redevelopment involving demolition and reconstruction or rehabilitation of existing housing, the routes of projected superhighways, and any other factual information that would indicate accelerated or decelerated movement of potential school population in the study area. In addition to these official sources, many local improvement groups and members of parent-teacher associations provided census data on children of preschool age which were very helpful in forecasting the urgency of need for a new facility. It was found that ratios computed between the data that could be statistically interrelated revealed patterns of growth and development that often were very stable and of great value as predictors of the future, so long as the basic conditions remained relatively unchanged. The use of a transparent overlay, on which was spotted by city block the home of each child according to the school which he attended, brought out the various aspects of the problem, and where more than one school was involved, several overlays were used on top of each other.

The study of population indexes helps to determine not only the approximate location of a future building or the enlargement of an existing building, but also the number of pupils it should accommodate. However, this number will not be the maximum that the curve of expected population might indicate, but something short of it, which will be sufficient to care for the peak load, perhaps with some temporary supplementary facilities, and after the peak has passed, to provide comfortable occupancy at a standard of approximately thirty pupils per classroom. This policy was adopted early in the program to prevent over-building in any area and to spread the available funds as far as possible.

Extensive population studies in connection with the problem of a rehabilitated and enlarged Southern High School were contributed by the principal and his faculty, and trend studies were made by the Bureau of Research on the growth population in South Baltimore, Locust Point, and in the Curtis Bay-Brooklyn area, the three sections of the city which the school serves. The studies also brought out the inadequacies of the existing Southern High School plant, especially for instruction in senior high subjects. Various community proposals for site development in the vicinity of Federal Hill Park and elsewhere were received and considered by the School Plant Planning Committee and by the School Board. Two centrally located sites were tentatively selected by the Board on recommendation of the School Plant Planning Committee but both of these locations after long delay proved untenable for various reasons. Finally, a compromise was reached by decision of the Board of School Commissioners to expand the facilities [1] at the present Southern High School and to erect as soon as feasible a small senior high school in the Brooklyn Hills area.

The colored schools in the heart of the city have felt the impact of the steady growth in pupil population most severely. Most of the schools which have felt the burden heaviest are in buildings which have been scheduled for replacement since the time of the Strayer survey in 1922.

---

[1] The new facilities were to include 19 classrooms, office suite, health suite, gymnasium and swimming pool to be erected on land to be secured immediately adjacent to the existing building.

PORTABLE CLASSROOMS, ALWAYS NEEDED IN LIMITED QUANTITIES BECAUSE OF SHIFTING POPULATION, CAN BE ATTRACTIVE AND EFFICIENT. THIS FACT IS DEMONSTRATED IN THE FIVE SPACIOUS, WELL LIGHTED, HEATED, AND VENTILATED CLASSROOMS AT SCHOOL NO. 153A, ERECTED IN 1949

Had the recommendations of the Survey Commission been carried out in previous years and a full quota of new classrooms erected each decade, pupils would have been decently housed, though not adequately. As it is, obsolescence, both educational and structural, and inadequacy create the need for many more structures than existing funds will allow. However, on this program a start was made on the problem of relief. The West Baltimore Colored Elementary School at Saratoga and Schroeder Streets was designed to help

TABLE 17

CLASSROOMS BUILT BY DECADES

Decade	Number
TOTAL:	2,894
Average	413
1880-89	279
1890-99	462
1900-09	301
1910-19	423
1920-29	787
1930-39	609
1940-49	33

reduce the load on existing West Baltimore buildings and perhaps to permit the closing of one of the oldest and worst buildings in that part of the city. A site for a new building was early secured at Barre and Warner Streets to replace and relieve schools in that general area. By the end of the year the future of this site had been put in jeopardy by the later projection of the Washington-Baltimore Freeway through one edge of the property. To relieve congestion in East Baltimore a site for a third building was located at Wolfe, Chase, and Washington Streets and its acquisition by the Real Estate Agency was begun.

TABLE 18
TYPES OF PORTABLE BUILDINGS ERECTED IN 1950

Type	School	Location	Description
FRAME	113A	1336 North Eden St.	3 classrooms, boys' toilet, girls' toilet, gas-fired furnaces, slimlined fluorescent lighting
	232A	North Athol Avenue near Edmondson Ave.	2 classrooms, boys' toilet, girls' toilet, gas-fired furnaces, slimlined fluorescent lighting
	233	Roland Avenue, near Deepdene Road	3 classrooms with corridor, no toilets, steam heating from a central plant, slimlined electric lighting
	234	Rogers and Magnolia Avenues	4 classrooms with corridor, steam heating from central plant, slimlined fluorescent lighting
METAL	122	Preston Street near Druid Hill Avenue	4 classrooms with corridor, steam heating from a central plant, slimlined fluorescent lighting
	152	Frankfurst Avenue and Rake Court	2 classrooms, oil-fired furnaces, slimlined fluorescent lighting
CEMESTO	112A	1343 North Calhoun Street	4 classrooms with corridor, boys' toilets, girls' toilets, gas-fired furnaces, slimlined fluorescent lighting
	138	Harlem Avenue and Monroe Street	1 building of 4 classrooms and corridor, 1 building of 2 classrooms without corridor, gas-fired furnaces, slimlined fluorescent lighting
	159	801 Bridgeview Ave. Cherry Hill	4 classrooms and corridor, gas-fired furnaces, slimlined fluorescent lighting

Portable Structures

When School No. 153, Holabird and Bob White Avenues, became badly congested and on part time, the School Plant Planning Committee decided to experiment with prefabricated buildings as a comparatively rapid means of relief on the assumption that portable structures could be attractive in appearence, reasonable in cost, and comfortable for occupancy. So successful was this original project that when the influx of new students in various parts of the city began to mount at excessive rates, the School Plant Planning Committee decided to recommend the erection of a relatively large number of such auxiliary structures at strategic locations.

The pioneer building at Holabird Avenue and Broening Highway, known as No. 153A, consisted of factory-built units, delivered to the site and erected on foundation work and floor supports put in place by the Department of Education. Panels for exterior walls and roof generally were six feet wide and of varying length. The floor panels were likewise six feet wide, and, in most cases, 24 feet long, the width of the classroom. The roofing was of asphalt strip shingles, and all walls and floors were insulated. Each of the five classroom units, corridor connected, contained a classroom 24 feet by 36 and a workroom 12 feet by 18. It was heated by a gas-fired furnace and lighted by cold cathode fluorescent fixtures.

The 1950 expanded program included four frame buildings, two all-metal, and three buildings with cemesto walls and metal roofs. The frame buildings were sectional, but in this instance the panels were eight feet wide, except the floor panels which remained at six feet. The metal buildings consisted of a sectional steel framework with trusses, purlins, girts, etc., and corrugated, insulated metal sheets for exterior walls, and a finished roof. The floors were wood panels, similar to the flooring used in the frame group. The cemesto buildings included structural steel frame and trusses, with purlins and girts. The exterior walls were

approximately 1⅝ inches thick erected with companion
extruded aluminum sections, the roof of corrugated metal.
Table 18 gives a description of the buildings erected of
: each type.

To relieve congestion and part time in the Curtis Bay
area the School Board also arranged with the Federal Housing Authority for the lease of six of their temporary housing units for reconditioning as classrooms for use in September, 1950.

Building and Community Studies

Under the leadership of its principal each elementary
school made a survey of its building and the community
which it serves. Central office personnel assisted in the
technical aspects of the problem, including the structural
condition of the building, population trends, and methods
for enlisting public cooperation and support in securing
basic survey data and in developing recommendations regarding the future school needs of the community.

The specific character of the data derived from these
studies and the interpretation supplied by the school and
its cooperating public furnishes a sound basis for future
planning. In developing its report practically every school
was able to obtain the assistance of parents and community
leaders in gathering basic information regarding probable
future school population, the activities of builders, and
the resources of the community. The outcome of this undertaking was a clearer understanding of school problems on
the part of the parents and members of the community
and a series of recommendations for building improvements which they could support. It provided the principal with that "long view" which is so necessary for the
most successful administration of a unit of the public
school system.

SERVICES IN THE INTERESTS OF
CHILDREN AND ADULTS

To enable children to gain maximum benefit from the educational opportunities which the city provides for them there is need for many individual services and for schools and classes of many types. To this end various opportunities for analysis and guidance have been organized through the years to help the child find the educational program best adapted to him. Other services enrich the classroom instruction directly, such as audio-visual aids, radio and television, and libraries. The work of a number of these services and some of the more significant achievements of the two-year period are described in detail below starting with the work of the Committee on Child Guidance and Adjustment, a system-wide committee whose function is to seek a better coordination of the various departments and activities of the Department of Education in the interests of the child.

Committee on Child Guidance and Adjustment

Appointed by the Superintendent in 1948, the Committee on Child Guidance and Adjustment during the past two years was engaged in the study of problems of child welfare in relation to the services provided by the Department of Education. In so doing the committee drew extensively on the experience of teachers, principals, and others, including lay groups and professional organizations. Some of the major fields which it explored are described below together with the tentative conclusions which were reached.

1. The problem of the slow-learner, especially in early adolescence, was heightened by the revised State school attendance law [1] which requires that all children, excepting a few who are excused for mental or physical reasons, shall

---

[1] Acts of the Maryland Legislature 1947; effective July 1, 1949.

attend school regularly until their sixteenth birthday. This law especially affected the large number of children between the ages of 14 and 16 who annually withdrew from school for purposes of gainful employment or to remain at home to engage in domestic duties. The committee accordingly devoted much time to a re-examination of the programs for boys and girls of these ages, especially the shop center and occupational classes, the junior high schools, and the general vocational schools, to determine the parts which met most effectively the identified needs of these pupils. It is expected that out of these studies will come stimulation for a wider application of these curricular adaptations and the development of other approaches that will give a sense of value to school work.

2. Early in the work of the committee, it was recognized that the effective adjustment of children at all levels of the school program depended very largely upon the creation and maintenance of sound personal relations between teacher and pupil. This problem was, in turn, related to the general tone of the relationships which exist among the administrative, supervisory, and instructional personnel on the staff. To secure a better understanding of the ways in which these aspects of the school program might be further improved, a survey was undertaken to identify successful practices in individual schools and to determine their applicability to other schools.

3. For a number of years, guidance in the elementary schools was limited to part-time service by counselors attached to neighboring junior high schools who spend a minor portion of their time in visits to elementary schools. An advisory subcommittee of persons experienced in elementary education and guidance was asked to evaluate the effectiveness of this program and to make recommendations. As a result, there was established in two elementary schools, one white and one colored, as of February 1, 1950, a program of full-time guidance. Experienced counselors with special qualifications for this work were selected and assigned. The advisory committee continued to keep in

close touch with the progress of the work. After one semester of trial, the results were found to be so satisfactory that arrangements were made to establish two additional centers in somewhat different types of communities beginning in September, 1950.

4.   One of the particularly pressing problems which gave rise to the appointment of the Committee on Child Guidance and Adjustment was the large number of pupils who leave school before the completion of any full program of instruction.   While economic and social problems play some part in the underlying causes, it has been established that most of the children who become drop-outs are those for whom school has meant a series of unsuccessful and unsatisfying experiences.   Usually boys and girls who leave school for this reason merely move on into an employment situation that differs only slightly, if at all, from what it was in school.   The committee was convinced that little improvement would be effected by attempting to deal with premature school-leaving as such, since this manifestation is essentially a symptom which appears only at a late stage of a serious educational condition.   The problem is to develop programs which will be likely to bring about worthwhile accomplishment and growth with satisfaction, for neither society nor the individual child is well served if, after ten or so years of education at public expense, large numbers of children are droppng out of school with a less than even chance for a satisfactory adjustment in terms of social or economic competence.

5.   The committee recognized a need for a well conceived and clearly expressed statement of the philosophy of education which underlies the work of the Baltimore Public Schools.   In a democracy such a statement is not passed down from some top agency or individual, but is attained on the basis of widespread participation, complete contribution, and collective evaluation.   Since the beginning of the committee's work, a subgroup has been engaged in reexamining the many statements which have been made from time to time by individual schools or divisions to

express their philosophy. Out of these pronouncements the committee seeks to formulate a comprehensive statement which will represent the philosophical basis upon which the entire system rests.

Guidance and Counseling Service

Guidance is the process of helping the student to plan his school and life career on the basis of his abilities, ambitions, and opportunities. It is the systematic study of

COUNSELOR AIDED BY THE PARENT ADVISES PUPIL'WHO THINKS
SHE NEEDS TO WITHDRAW FROM SCHOOL

the student by himself and by his counselors, including his teachers. The impact of the guidance function upon the pupil begins in the elementary school and extends throughout his entire school career. With the counselor groups of pupils visit industry and business. Motion pictures of the world of work are brought to the classroom. Representatives of various occupations meet with interested groups of pupils in the school to discuss the opportunities in their respective fields, the educational requirements for admission, and the working conditions which generally prevail. The full scope of this service is de-

:scribed in the issue of the *Baltimore Bulletin of Education* for April-May, 1949.

The periodic studies of the Department of Guidance and Placement provide basic data for the use of teacher, coun- :selor, curriculum committee, and school administrator. Its 1950 report of withdrawals shows that of the non-objective reasons for withdrawal (that is, when physical disability, marriage, removal from the city or entering the armed forces are excluded) dislike of school, whether expressed as failure, indifference, discipline, a desire to go to work, or the mere fact of being over the compulsory school at- tendance age, constitutes the major reason for school leav- ing. The principal withdrawal trends for reasons other than removal from city were found to be as follows:

1. In the high schools the heaviest incidence of withdrawal took place in the tenth grade (52.6%), with less than half as many in the eleventh grade (34.3%).

2. Nearly 70 per cent of pupils who left were unsuccessful in their work as shown by their school marks.

3. In the junior high schools for colored pupils, the per cent of pupils withdrawing from the eighth grade was the highest (47.6%), followed by the seventh (28.6%) and the ninth (23.8%).

4. In the junior high schools for white pupils, the principal leav- ing grade was the ninth (44.2%), with the eighth (33.9%) and the seventh (21.9%) trailing.

5. Of the junior high leavers, 5.2% of the colored students and 7.9% of the white students were over 17½ years of age, which reveals retardation and its attendant problems.

Graduates are followed one year after graduation. A report of the findings of this investigation is contained ·in the Statistical Section of this report.

Placement—Pupils who complete their public schooling are assisted in finding appropriate jobs through the Place- ment Service. The number of jobs listed by employers dur- ing the past two years and a summary of the requirements set for these will be found in the Statistical Section. The tables reveal the trends in employment for beginning workers in Baltimore. The principal characteristics of these trends up to June 30, 1950 may be summarized as follows:

1. Employers were becoming increasingly selective. They were insisting that their applicants be high school graduates, be proficient in their skills, make a pleasing appearance and have an attractive manner. Many firms were administering tests in arithmetic and English to help them select the best possible workers.

2. The number of employer requests for clerical workers greatly exceeded those received for either technical jobs or employment in industry.

3. It took longer for the beginning worker to obtain employment, particularly if he were interested in locating a specific type of job.

4. Typists with good computational ability and operators for specialized jobs such as the comptometer and bookkeeping machines were in great demand.

5. From July 1949 through February 1950, the requests for boys declined. However, this situation changed somewhat during the later months when more requests were received during May and June of 1950 than for the same period of 1949.

6. The new labor law requiring the payment of a minimum wage of 75c an hour for all employees of companies that engage in interstate commerce brought about high school graduation as a prerequisite for many jobs previously filled by non-graduates and a rise in salaries for all types of clerical work to an average of $30 per week.

Services to Adults—Since 1945 a counseling service for adults has been maintained to provide help for individuals in long-term educational planning, evaluation of credits toward graduation requirements, requirements for entrance to college or to some vocational opportunity, curriculum adjustment or the interpretation of test results. During the period from July 1, 1949 to July 1, 1950, the two counselors in this field conducted 5,087 interviews and answered 1,777 inquiries by mail and 5,629 by telephone.

Rehabilitation Service

For the physically handicapped pupils of the public schools—principally from the William S. Baer and the

Francis M. Wood schools—there is provided upon withdrawal, and without charge, a service of guidance and
vocational training that will, in time, fit them for remunera-
tive employment in work that they can do proficiently. This
service is made possible by the Division of Vocational Rehabilitation of the State Department of Education through
a specialist jointly employed by that division and the Division of Special Education of the Department of Education.   His assignment includes service as counselor at
the William S. Baer and the Francis M. Wood schools for
physically handicapped. To him are referred the graduates

TABLE 19

AMOUNTS EXPENDED IN STATE REHABILITATION PROGRAM FOR
PHYSICALLY HANDICAPPED PUPILS OF BALTIMORE

Item	1948-49	1949-50
TOTAL EXPENDITURE	$11,350	$13,505
Diagnostic medical examinations	500	185
Medical and surgical treatment	400	1,040
Prosthesis	400	625
Tuition for vocational training	8,000	7,800
Maintenance of clients in training	1,600	3,150
Transportation of clients in training	50	265
Training supplies and equipment	400	440

and former students of these schools as well as cases in
need of rehabilitation that are reported by counselors and
nurses in other schools.

Training programs are developed on the basis of detailed interviews supplemented by diagnostic information
obtained from medical examinations, psychological testing,
scholastic and other pertinent records.   Each year over
one hundred clients begin some type of vocational training
in public schools, in private trade schools, business colleges,
regular colleges or in professional schools.   During the
training period the specialist has at least two contacts with
each of the 360 or more persons on his roll.   Many are in-

terviewed more frequently at their homes, in school, or at their place of employment. More than half of them receive their training in public schools or in some other educational institution without additional cost to the division. For the others tuition in whole or in part is paid from public funds. In a few cases in which financial need was established, the division paid the tuition and in addition the cost of one or more of the following: supplies and equipment, maintenance, and transportation. Most clients are reported by school counselors and nurses at age 16 or younger, and their cases are not closed until several years later, after their training has been completed.

The principal costs of the service are borne by the Division of Vocational Rehabilitation, State Department of Education. A breakdown of these costs for each of the two years covered by this report is shown in Table 19. In each of these years 42 clients were declared rehabilitated. Since approximately $3,000 was spent on the group completing their training in 1948-49, the cost per rehabilitated client amounted to a little less than $72.00. As this group of clients earned in wages slightly over $29.00 a week, they had earned an amount equal to the cost of their rehabilitation in 2½ weeks. The 1949-50 group was more expensive: their total cost of training was approximately $9,600, or an average of nearly $230 per rehabilitated client. Earning an average of slightly over $28.00 per week in wages, they required eight weeks to equal the cost of their rehabilitation.

Measurement Services

Standardized tests are to the educative process what instruments are to the aviator or engineer. They serve as guides in adapting the school program to the needs of each child. They help the teacher to discover what progress a child is making from year to year and whether he is achieving up to what may reasonably be expected of him in terms of his apparent capacity and effort. Test results also reveal how well a child is achieving as compared with his peers. Both types of evaluation are important in a child's life and program of education. The data which they yield are basic to good teaching, sound diagnosis, and effective counseling.

City-wide Testing Program—Over 100,000 tests were administered by the Bureau of Research to elementary school children during the current year; nearly 22,000 to secondary school pupils. The chief purpose of the testing program continues to be the measurement, with as much accuracy as possible, of each child's academic aptitude (the capacity to do school work as measured by standardized tests) and, at frequent intervals, of his achievement in various school subjects, particularly in the ability to read and in the mastery of arithmetical processes. The testing program for many years has furnished objective measurements of each child's progress, thereby facilitating an intelligent program of instruction. While full recognition is given to teachers' opinions of the progress that the pupils make in school, these judgments become more and more trustworthy to the extent that they are based on objective evidence.

Psychometric Services—Whenever there are children who seem to be maladjusted educationally, they may be referred to the Psychoeducational Clinic for detailed study. The principal supplies the child's school history, the school doctor makes the necessary physical examination, and the clinic administers one or more individual intelligence tests as may be needed. During the year 1949-50 over 3,700 children ranging in age from 3 to 21 years when tested, and in grade from prekindergarten to 11B, were examined in the clinic. Although most of the cases were referred directly by the schools, the clinic also received some from other divisions of the Department of Education, principally the Division of Special Services (712 in 1949-50) and the Reading Clinic (603 in 1949-50).

A large percentage of the children referred to the clinic were mentally handicapped, but some were physically handicapped, and others were emotionally disturbed. Distributions of intelligence quotients obtained during a nine-

TABLE 20

SCOPE OF TESTING PROGRAM ADMINISTERED BY THE
BUREAU OF RESEARCH

Subjects, Grades and Time of Testing	1948-1949			1949-1950		
	Total	White	Colored	Total	White	Colored
TOTAL TESTS	150,756	98,045	52,711	137,370	88,917	48,453
Total Elementary	108,967	67,525	41,442	93,735	57,678	36,057
Intelligence						
September, 2B, 2A [1], 4B, 4A [1]	20,187	12,768	7,419	14,640	9,061	5,579
February, 2B, 4B	7,826	4,780	3,046	8,049	5,056	2,993
Reading						
September, 3B-6A	38,183	24,128	14,055	38,902	24,219	14,683
Sept., Special Ed.	2,473	1,261	1,212	2,299	1,207	1,092
Occupational	1,499	858	641	1,501	895	606
Shop Centers	1,511	745	766	1,496	740	756
Arithmetic						
Sept., 3B [2], 3A [2], 4A-6A	31,839	20,110	11,729	21,578	13,673	7,905
Sept., Occupational	1,491	857	634	1,496	892	604
Special	2,462	1,259	1,203	2,290	1,199	1,091
Shop Centers	1,496	759	737	1,484	736	748
Total Secondary	41,789	30,520	11,269	43,635	31,239	12,396
Intelligence						
September, 7B	4,462	3,172	1,290	4,849	3,434	1,415
February, 7B	2,698	1,750	948	2,951	1,973	978
Reading [3]						
September, 7B, 9B......	8,047	5,994	2,053	7,724	5,510	2,214
February, 7B, 9B........	4,142	2,887	1,255	4,987	3,384	1,603
Arithmetic						
September, 7B, 8A [4]....	4,412	3,153	1,259	7,030	4,914	2,116
February, 7B, 8A........	....	....	....	6,710	4,673	2,038
English						
September, 7B	4,396	3,151	1,245	....	....	....
Spelling						
September, 7B	4,392	3,151	1,241	....	....	....
Intelligence						
September, 10B	3,041	2,509	532	3,134	2,545	589
February, 10B	1,582	1,143	439	1,825	1,367	458
Reading						
September, 10B	3,066	2,506	560	2,781	2,194	587
February, 10B	1,551	1,104	447	1,644	1,246	398

[1] This test was not given to Grades 2A and 4A in 1949-50.
[2] This test was not given to Grades 3B and 3A in 1949-50.
[3] As of February, 1949, Grade 9B reading tests were optional.
[4] Grade 8A was not tested in 1948-49.

year period are remarkably uniform, with a tendency in the past few years toward a larger proportion of brighter pupils being referred for testing.

Individual performance tests were administered for speech defects, severe hearing handicaps, and foreign language handicaps. Of special significance is the increasing interest on the part of principals and teachers in the interpretation of the results of the testing. This trend indicates a growing awareness of the psychological im-

TABLE 21

PERCENT OF CASES REFERRED TO PSYCHOEDUCATIONAL CLINIC
AT VARIOUS LEVELS

Range of Intelligence Quotients	1948-49	1949-50	Nine Year Average
110 and above	4	6	4
90 to 109	20	29	19
50 to 89 [1]	74	63	75
Under 50 [2]	2	2	2

[1] The opportunity and shop center classes are recruited from this area.
[2] For children in this area, education in a public school is difficult and in many cases questionable.

plications of mental measurement and its relation to the child as a whole. It is especially important for them to be conscious of the phenomenon of pseudo-feeblemindedness. Sensory defects such as unidentified hearing, visual, speech, muscular coordination and emotional impairments, singly or in combination, create the appearance of feeblemindedness. Genuine clinical psychology can identify and help these children by pointing the way to the treatment which such children require to permit the growth of their native intelligence.

Aptitude Testing—The service of aptitude testing is based on the realization that valid, objective information, properly interpreted, will condition and justify any recommendation that can be made in advising the student on his educational and developmental program. Its introduction and extension have been initiated as a result of the many problems faced by those who come in direct contact with children.

A number of years ago, through careful research in the field of scholastic prediction, a battery of tests was worked out which would be of assistance in advising graduating high school students as to the selection of a college and also areas of specialization on the college level. This battery reflected interest, capacity in scientific areas, and capacity in technical or engineering areas. After being administered to a large number of veterans and many high school seniors, it proved to be of considerable value in counseling on the college entrance level. During the year, 1949-50, all public high school graduates making application for the teachers' colleges and the Baltimore Junior College were tested and advised on the basis of their achievement on the test battery.

A series of tests was developed in connection with the work-study program in two senior high schools. The tests were given before the work-study training period and their results provided the basis for an intensive review and remedial program instituted to prepare the students for employment. Considerable success was reported by the commercial department in up-grading and in placing students as a result of this testing-training program.

Two batteries of tests, one for boys and one for girls, were developed as entrance tests for the skilled trade courses. Their use was expanded to the survey level for junior and senior high school students in the choice of vocational, technical, and other curricula requiring mechanical and clerical aptitude.

A small committee, in cooperation with the Business Education Department, is working on the problem of establishing on-the-job criteria for success. This will permit a procedure for establishing the validity of the tests for the business department on actual job progress.

While the stenographic battery has been of considerable help in advising students as to their relative success in the stenographic courses, it is necessary that other courses in the commercial areas be considered. A student may be unsuited for stenography, but at the same time may have characteristics which could be used to his advantage in courses other than stenography in the business field. For this reason, a differential battery for stenography, machine operation, typewriting and general business practice has been under consideration. The outcome will be a single battery of tests which can be used for guidance purposes in advising the student as to his opportunities in any of the above-named courses.

The sources and types of cases referred to the Department of Aptitude Testing are shown in the detailed table in the Statistical Section of this report.

Division of Special Services

In any large school system there are many children who present problems of maladjustment to the school situation, usually expressed in terms of aggressive behavior and irregular attendance. Such cases are referred to the Division of Special Services for Pupils where, in consultation with parents, and on the basis of home visits and other technical aids and of psychological and psychiatric tests administered by trained personnel in the division or in some outside clinic, a constructive plan of action is developed which promises improvement. Each case is assigned to a visiting teacher who becomes the child's friend and counselor in carrying out the several steps of the plan.

The total number of cases active during 1949-50 in the Division of Special Services was 3,601, which represents 3.1 per cent of the total school population. Most authorities estimate that at least 5 per cent of the children in the schools need the service which the division provides

489707

and, therefore, it seems likely that many cases which could be helped still are not being referred by the schools. However, when taken over a five-year period there has been a slow but steady increase in the referral rate. Moreover, about four times as many children were referred to the division during the current year for behavior manifestations as there were in 1944-1945 with a corresponding decrease in referrals for absence and truancy, which are usually taken to be but symptoms of a more important maladjustment.

The median age of the referred cases, while remaining at thirteen years, was considerably higher than it should be for most effective treatment. The trend in age, however, is downward, which is a source of satisfaction because it gives a longer period for remedial action. The median IQ is still considerably below 100, but there has been a relatively larger number of cases which by reason of good intelligence present favorable possibilities for adjustment.

The proportion of cases showing improvement by the close of the year maintained a steady average of about 60 per cent. This ratio compares very favorably with the proportion reported by clinics and agencies which restrict their intake to a small number of cases and to those which give good promise of response. There are no restrictions on intake in the Division of Special Services.

A study made during the year 1950 by a committee consisting of three members of the Board of School Commissioners and three staff members appointed by the president of the Board began with a survey of existing services in the division and concluded with a number of recommendations for future expansion. This report was published in full in the Minutes of the Board of School Commisioners of June 1, 1950. Among the recommendations were increased psychiatric,[2] psychological, and visiting teacher service; adjustment of the ratio of home visitors to visit-

---

[2] The committee recommended that this expansion be in terms of part-time personnel because of the larger number available and the value of their outside experience.

ing teachers; increased clinical [3] service; increased office space, particularly the provision of private interviewing rooms; and the addition of another supervisor of visiting teacher service. In accordance with these recommendations an increase of staff was authorized to include two psychologists, full-time; four psychiatrists, part-time; and three additional visiting teachers, raising their number to 22.

Reading Clinic

Since the initiation of Reading Clinic service in September, 1945, the program has expanded to six clinics with three reading specialists and eight expert teachers of reading. This expansion involved the in-service training of four persons preparatory to the opening of three reading clinics in occupational and junior high schools. For pupils in the occupational classes clinics were established in September, 1949 at School No. 98A, Ashton and Smallwood Streets, and No. 116A on Aisquith Street near Lexington, for white and colored pupils respectively.

TABLE 22

READING CLINICS, 1948-1950

Service Rendered	1948-49	1949-50
Number of clinics in operation............................	3	6
Number of referrals studied in clinic..............	176	239
Enrollment, instructional division......................	122	179
Average case load per clinic...............................	20	17
Average monthly gain per pupil......................	1.5	1.8
Number discharged	89	137

The clinic at School No 79, Park Avenue and Hoffman Street, was opened on February 1, 1950 for pupils in that school, but beginning in September, 1950 its services were to be made available to junior high students throughout

---

[3] This recommendation was based on the fact that community psychiatric service had become practically nonexistent, hence the need for departmental staff.

the system.   Pupils in need of reading clinic services were
to transfer to School No. 79, Park Avenue and Hoffman
Street, after being tested at the clinic in the term preceding the expected transfer. To qualify for the clinical service their chronological age must be 14-6 or less at time of
referral; their standardized reading score at least two
years below grade level, and their IQ, based upon a
Stanford-Binet test administered within two years of referral to the clinic, 85 or higher.

Remedial reading service of a clinical character is now
available at elementary, occupational, and junior high levels.
Table 22 outlines the scope and accomplishment of this
service.

Radio and Television

As a means of promoting a better understanding of public school policies and providing learning situations of
genuine interest to students, radio and television have
been used throughout the school system for some years
in cooperation with the local radio stations.   Four regularly scheduled programs were in operation throughout
1949-50.

1. "School Reporter," WBMD, Saturdyas at 10:25 A.M., a five-
   minute weekly program featuring news about schools, written
   and presented by students. It ran from September 17 through
   June 17, 38 programs.

2. "Your Baltimore Schools," WFBR, Tuesdays 6:45 P.M., a ten-
   minute program utilizing both the dramatic and discussion
   formats, November 1 to June 30, 29 programs, 234 participants.

3. "Junior Town Meeting," WBAL, Wednesdays 9:30 A.M., a
   thirty-minute program on current issues in and out of schools,
   in which ten high schools and the Baltimore Junior College
   participated.

4. "News Clinic," WCBM, Saturdays 2:15 P.M. and 4:15 P.M., a
   fifteen-minute program conducted in cooperation with Mr.
   Greg Halpin of WCBM. For eight Saturdays students interested in the operations involved in gathering, transmitting, editing, and broadcasting the news assembled at WCBM for a talk
   on newscasting by Mr. Halpin. This decision was followed by
   an actual news broadcast by the students.

In addition to the four regularly scheduled programs, occasional programs of local interest were organized from time to time.

THE SUPERINTENDENT'S NEWSLETTER PROVIDES A MEDIUM FOR REPORTS AND ANNOUNCEMENT OF FUTURE EVENTS OF INTEREST TO MEMBERS OF THE DEPARTMENT OF EDUCATION

A new medium of instruction and public understanding, television, was inaugurated in 1950. In February, "Baltimore Classroom—1950," a series showing classes at work, gave parents an opportunity to observe just what goes

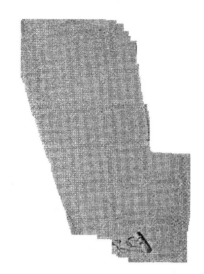

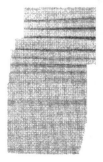

on in school. Classroom furniture and equipment, children, and teachers were all transported to WAAM-TV every Friday, for the half-hour presentation of "Baltimore Classroom" at 7:00 P.M. Teachers taught unrehearsed lessons and children's reactions were natural and spontaneous. This series met with an enthusiastic reception from parents, teachers, children, and the public generally. So far as known, the Baltimore Department of Education was the only school system that was presenting such a program at that time. Fifteen programs featured 17 teachers and approximately 450 pupils.

The year 1950 also marked the beginning of experimental teaching by television. For this experiment Station WBAL-TV provided time on Thursdays from 2:00 to 2:50 for lessons at both elementary and secondary level: *For the elementary schools,* five lessons on how to play melody instruments, one lesson on safety, two library [4] lessons; *for the secondary schools,* three social studies lessons, four aviation lessons, two guidance lessons. Over 9,100 pupils in school observed the lessons by means of sets which were loaned to the school for this purpose. As a result of this experiment the possibilities of television were deemed well worth further exploration.

School Libraries

Enlarged appropriations in the budget of the Department of Education for additional personnel, books, and equipment made possible improvement in library services in many schools. Eleven librarians were appointed during 1949-50 to serve sixteen elementary schools which had libraries but no librarian and two junior high schools. Thus by the end of June, 1950 there were 29 buildings with full-time libraries; 16 buildings with libraries and part-time library service; 38 schools that had a library the size of a classroom but no librarian; 35 that had a

---

[4] The first was devoted to the development of a book, from the author's idea through the manuscript stage, various steps in editing and printing, to the completed book. The second lesson included the methods of illustrating the book and the steps necessary in binding a book.

central depository smaller than a classroom and no librarian; and 31 with classroom libraries only. The total
school library book collection for the city stood at 210,384.
Although there was a one-per-cent gain in the total book
collections during the biennium, the average number of
library books available per pupil per school fell far below
the five books per pupil deemed necessary by the American
Library Association for an adequate school library. For
the city as a whole the average number of library books

TABLE 23

SCHOOL LIBRARY BOOKS AVAILABLE PER PUPIL, JUNE, 1950

Library Staff	Schools With Libraries	Total Books	Average Pupils	Books Per Pupil
TOTAL:	149	210,384	112,790	1.9
School librarian, elementary............	20	24,590	16,006	1.5
School librarian, junior high [1]........	14	36,283	17,626	2.0
School librarian, senior high [2]..........	10	45,974	18,070	2.5
School librarian, el.-teachers coll....	1	1,905	870	2.0
Central depository only, classroom	38	48,462	28,351	1.7
Central depository only, small........	35	20,366	20,045	1.0
Classroom libraries only....................	31	15,546	11,822	1.3
Library books in classrooms [3]..........	....	17,258	....	......

[1] Includes junior high schools with an elementary division and one general vocational school.
[2] Includes one vocational high school, the junior college, and senior high schools
with a junior high division.
[3] Classroom collections of library books in schools which also have a central library.

per pupil was less than two. The ratio varies by educational level and by type of library service, as will be seen
from Table 23. For schools having librarians, the range
extended from a low of .69 to a high of 4.01. The elementary schools ranged from a low of .69 to a high of 3.6; and
the secondary schools from a low of .9 to a high of 4.01.
This was the first year that a complete survey on the book
collections in the several schools was made.

Through the Equipment Loan new library units were installed and in other libraries such items as new shelving, book trucks, vertical files, dictionary stands, typewriters, tables and chairs, display racks, newspaper racks, step stools, librarians' desks or cases for card catalogs were supplied. In some schools the librarian's working space was entirely rearranged. All this equipment made it possible for the library to increase its efficiency, provide for a larger book stock, improve the organization of its materials, appear more attractive, and give better service to both teachers and pupils.

Audio-Visual Aids

The function of purchase, distribution, and maintenance of audio-visual aids and instruction in their use is centered in the Division of Audio-Visual Education. In addi-

TABLE 24

NEW AUDIO-VISUAL EQUIPMENT SECURED THROUGH EQUIPMENT LOAN

Description	Number Purchased
Projectors—motion picture, slide, filmstrip	44
Prints of sound motion pictures	1686
Filmstrips (8 with sound)	1721
Flat pictures, slides ....sets	194
Phonograph records ....sets	136
Record players, dual speed	5
Recorders, tape and disc	4
Portable public address systems	2

tion to administering the machinery of distribution, the division provides a technical and consultant service for principals who are contemplating new installations or additional equipment, individual instruction in the use of projection equipment, and a general informational service which is often rendered through faculty conferences and the meetings of special groups such as the probationary teachers and members of parent-teacher associations. As a matter of good public relations the division gives as much technical service as possible to outside organizations which call for information, guidance, and practical assistance in their audio-visual programs.

Never before have the scope and variety of aids available in the division come as near meeting the needs of modern teaching as they were at the end of the current year. This happy condition was the direct outcome of the School Equipment Loan which made possible the extensive purchases summarized in Table 24. These acquisitions are made on the recommendation of the departments concerned, with whom films, prints, and records are always previewed before being placed in circulation. These contacts enable the division to keep abreast of changes in courses of study and of the subject matter that can best be taught by audio-visual materials.

IV

INSTRUCTIONAL POLICIES

Since 1946 approximately 1,200 teachers in Baltimore City have been participants in a program of child study directed by the staff of the Institute for Child Study at the University of Maryland. Beginning with directed study of one child, the recording of anecdotal material, drawing hypotheses, spotting recurring themes, and summarizing the record, the program in its three-year cycle developed objective scrutiny of behavior in place of subjective interpretation, and the cultivation of teacher-pupil and teacher-parent relationships on a level of mutual helpfulness. What is done for and with children, as well as what is not done, is guided by a consideration of the factors that influence children's behavior in the classroom, on the playground, in the home, and in the community outside of home and school. The comments of teachers and principals reveal the value of this program to teachers in their professional relationships. As they have had opportunity to clarify their concepts about children through discussion in child study classes, increasing rapport between teachers and parents has been observed.

The Child Study program continues to attract teachers who are interested in wholesome adjustment for children so that learning can proceed without undue impediment. During 1949-50, approximately 460 teachers were enrolled in first, second, third, and advanced child study groups. More and more teachers who have acquired some background of understanding of human development are rendering real service as members of groups that are concerned with improving the curriculum. This practical application of the principles of the Child Study program is probably a fundamental test of its value. The curriculum constantly feels this impact since teachers are looking more critically at the learning process and are analyzing more carefully individual problems in learning as a result of their experiences and training in the program.

Finally, the permeating of the child study point of view has had significant impact upon administrative policy, primarily in such areas as standards of promotion, reports to parents, cumulative records, and guidance.

Emerging Promotional Policies

It has become increasingly clear that "to teach children and not subjects" requires smaller classes and careful adaptation of instruction to the developmental stage of the pupils that compose the class.   Thus the standard of promotion becomes what is best *for him* and *for her,* and not a set amount of subject matter to be mastered.   During his schooling, the child grows continuously both mentally and physically.   Research has proven that many things are learned merely through the process of maturation and that holding children back often does more damage than good.   Studies have shown that to cause a pupil to repeat a grade does not eliminate the troubles of the child; it merely transfers the problem in an intensified form from one grade to another.   The *continuous growth plan* is an attempt to adjust an educational system to the total needs of the child so that he may be offered such opportunities for growth and development as are attainable by one of his intelligence; and it means, further, that his growth is to be measured, not alone by comparison with a group of pupils of widely varying inherited abilities, but also by his personal attainments as they reflect his innate capacities. It does not mean that all pupils are "passed" regardless of achievement, as later figures will show. It means, rather, that changes in curriculum planning and an improved system of guidance combine to offer the equality of educational opportunity to which every child is entitled; it means that more discretion—and more work—is left to the teacher in deciding what grade placement offers the best chance of progress for the individual child.

The new practices in the grading and promotion of pupils are based on the recognition of the individual character-istics of the child rather than on arbitrary standards fixed for a group. Every child who works up to the limit of his total capabilities is considered to be making satisfactory progress and is reasonably assured of promotion. It is only when his characteristics and responses vary widely from those of the other members of his group that there might be a decision not to promote him. The sound bases for promotion are the usual objective and subjective methods of measuring knowledge and skills, plus the teacher's estimate of the child's ability and his progress in all of the areas of the child development. The newer system of promotion recognizes both in theory and in practice that children of the same age differ. They are inferior or superior with respect to their progress in the various subjects in the curriculum. They vary in mental and physical maturity, in social and emotional development, in interests and attitudes, in talents and aptitudes. Because of the inevitable differences in the characteristics of the children of any group, the child's total progress must be judged on an individual basis, and the appraisal of that progress must include the whole front of child development.

Reporting to Parents

When the concept of continuous growth and development was accepted as basic in the instructional program, the inadequacies of the methods currently in use for reporting progress became apparent. During 1949, not less than seventy elementary schools had enlisted the cooperation of parents, teachers, and in many cases pupils, in attacking this problem of improving ways of recording and reporting pupil progress. Because of the spread of this experimentation throughout the city, the various proposals became a matter of far-reaching public interest. There was, consequently, a considerable amount of newspaper discussion, including feature articles devoted to the different kinds of report cards which had been developed by the various schools and to the reaction of parents to the newer procedures. A great number of parent-teacher association meetings were also devoted to a consideration of this educational problem.

A subcommittee of the Board of School Commissioners, Dr. Elizabeth Morrissy and Dr. J. Ben Robinson, was appointed to study the matter, to consider questions which had been raised, and to make recommendations and suggestions. This committee made a careful study of the problems of promotion and the means employed for keeping parents informed as to the progress of their children; it considered the underlying theories on which promotional practices were based and observed the conditions in the schools where those theories were then being applied. It examined the operations of the local system against the backgrounds of expert opinion of leading educators on the national level and of the success of the newer methods in national practices. It appraised the results achieved in the Baltimore schools under the *continuous growth practice* as they were reflected in the progress of the children during the past two years, and it compared the results with those formerly achieved under the traditional *grade standard practice*. As a consequence of this study the committee was convinced that the changes which were made were based on sound educational philosophy; that, because of the manner in which the Baltimore schools were gradually putting the new program into operation with the consent and cooperation of teachers and parents, there was general satisfaction with it; that the operation of the program is eminently successful in achieving its purpose of a well-rounded education for the child so as to fit him for living effectively in a highly complex society; and that the program improves the educational advantages of all the children without in the least diminishing the special opportunities of those who anticipate entrance into the curriculums of higher education, including the professions. It was the judgment of the committee that the Board of School Commissioners give its sanction to the new program by extending to the Board of School Superintendents, to the principals, and to the teachers of the Baltimore Public School System a vote of complete confidence.

The Board of School Commissioners in session on April 7, 1949 accepted the committee's report with thanks and unanimously approved its recommendations of confidence.

This period of exploration and the comments of parents and of the public proved exceedingly fruitful. They laid a basis for the work of the large city-wide committee of thirty-three principals, supervisors, specialists, and sixteen parents to which was given the task of designing a report card for use by all of the schools. A major strength of the committee lay in the fact that it represented every shade of opinion from the very conservative point of view which desired numerical grades to the extreme position which believed that parent-teacher conferences should replace the report card. The tentative form of report that evolved thus represented convictions that arose from extended discussion and the merging of conflicting points of view. Its salient characteristics were its emphasis upon evaluation of ability in terms of the child himself rather than in comparison with others; its recognition of stages of growth rather than marks of achievements as such; its adequate provisions for teacher and parent comments; its treatment of growth in the social and emotional areas as of equal rank with progress in the subject areas; and its interpretation of the school program to the parents.

The new report cards were available for service in the elementary schools in the city in the fall of 1949. In May, 1950, a divisional conference of parents, teachers, and principals attempted to evaluate the year's use of the new form of report card. A parent-opinion survey on a city-wide basis also formed a part of the discussion. The survey and the views expressed by parents and principals indicated that parents generally were in favor of the new report cards. They liked especially the opportunity afforded for comments by the teacher and for the parent's reply. They seemed to like the emphasis upon the child's progress with respect to his own abilities and a fuller reporting on many items of growth rather than the giving of marks in a few subjects. They appreciated the evidence gained from the new report cards that the teachers were studying the child carefully. The question of emphasizing competition through the report cards received considerable comment. There was divided opinion regarding the use of marks, with some indication that perhaps the majority of parents felt that a child should compete on the basis of his own abilities rather than on grade comparisons.

In the meantime, a subcommittee of the general committee on child guidance and adjustment was studying the city-wide system of cumulative records which accompany the child from school to school to determine what changes should be made so that the record form might serve more adequately not only each successive teacher but also counselors, employers, and schools of higher education. The objective of the committee was the development of a form which is mechanically efficient, which will reflect in consistent terms the child's educational growth throughout his entire school career, and will contain all of the information regarding the child that may be desired while he is still in school or after his separation from the school system.

Music in the Secondary Schools

During the two years covered by this report, the music program in the secondary schools was greatly expanded and enriched by the addition of major courses in both vocal and instrumental music in each academic high school except the Baltimore Polytechnic Institute and the appointment of a full-time teacher of instrumental music and several teachers of vocal music to each school. The availability of these vocal and instrumental teachers has meant the curricularizing of many music activities which formerly could be attempted only on a voluntary basis after school, and therefore the attainment of greater perfection of detail.

Vocal Music—Up to 1948 the teaching of vocal music in secondary schools was confined to one period of required music for all students, grades ten through twelve. Vocal music classes which meet five periods a week bear little resemblance to the extracurricular activities which supplemented the one curricular period but had to rely pri-

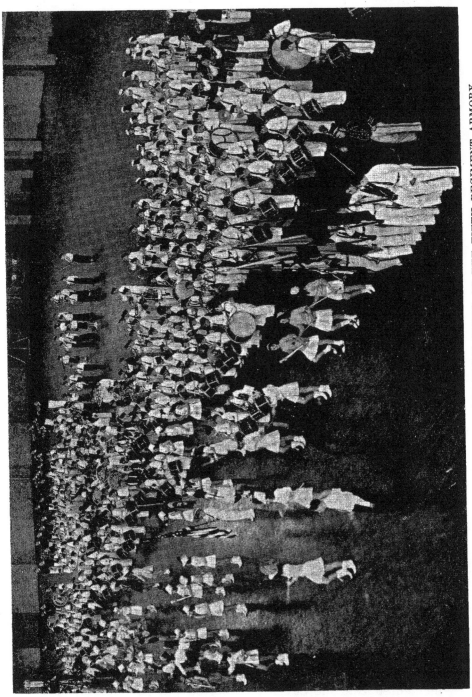

THE FESTIVAL OF BANDS AND DRUM CORPS AT THE FIFTH REGIMENT ARMORY

marily on a free-will offering of time and effort on the part of both students and teachers. The members of the elective music classes are brought in contact with music of complex form and content. There is sufficient time in the daily rehearsal to cultivate the individual capacity of each singer and to acquaint the group with some of the fine examples of choral music literature.

Most senior high schools were quick to develop choral music groups, identified by name, which show every indication of having permanent life within the school. The personnel may change from time to time as classes graduate, but a tradition of fine choral singing is growing.

Instrumental Music—Under the new program of instruction in band and orchestral instruments on a five-times-a-week basis rapid improvement in calibre of performance on music of higher quality and greater difficulty was observed in school functions and at the Annual Band and Orchestral Festival in March, 1950.

For the elementary and junior high levels a sequential program on a city-wide basis was inaugurated in September, 1949, starting in the fourth grade and continuing through the twelfth grade. To provide these expanded services in both elementary and secondary schools, the instrumental music staff was extended to eight full-time senior high instrumental teachers, seven full-time zone [1] teachers, one full-time elementary school string teacher, two part-time instrumental instructors, and two part-time drum and bugle instructors. The success of the program in its first year was due not only to the skill of the music teachers but in very large measure to the interest and support of each of the schools. Instruction was given in school time, requiring the arrangement of special schedules so that students might engage in instrumental activities. The number of such students was augmented by the fact that the purchase of several hundred clarinets, trumpets, and violins through the Equipment Loan made it possible

[1] A zone in the music division consists of one or two high schools and several adjacent elementary schools.

for hundreds of elementary school pupils to explore their interests and talents in instrumental music.

Recognition for Young Baltimore Artists

For several years vocational opportunities in art have been provided through major courses and the art curriculum in the senior high schools. The major courses were planned for those students who, having some ability, are interested in art as an avocation. The art curriculum enrolls students who look forward to continuing their study of art after graduation and hope ultimately to make some branch of art their life's work. Instruction is provided in general art, art appreciation, costume design and illustration, advertising design and architecture, painting, sculpture, industrial art, commercial art, and theater art. In addition to the opportunities in the senior high school courses in commercial art, sign painting, graphic arts, and general design are offered in the vocational high schools.

National Recognition—Sixty students of the Baltimore public schools were awarded keys at school assemblies for works submitted in the regional exhibition of the Scholastic Magazine Art Awards in 1950. More than 2,000 items had been submitted for this exhibit by art students throughout the State of Maryland. Of the 251 receiving honorable mention, 137 were pupils of the Baltimore public schools.

Out of the many thousands of examples of creative art produced in the high schools of the United States in 1950, which came before the juries at Carnegie Institute in Pittsburgh, only about 1,400 pieces of work were selected for a place in the National High School Art Exhibition. Of this number, twenty were from Baltimore public junior, vocational high, and senior high schools.

For its recently assembled collection of art works by children of North America the Worcester, Massachusetts, Art Museum in 1950 selected ten drawings and paintings done by pupils in the various grades from one up to senior high school. This collection of children's drawings and paintings was later made available on loan to museums and school systems throughout North America.

BAKING KILNS ENABLE CHILDREN TO EXPERIENCE ALL THE
PROCESSES OF MAKING CERAMICS

The fifty best pictures from schools in seventeen states in the Eastern Area were sent to the National Red Cross Headquarters to constitute a traveling exhibit to be used in the United States. Nine of the fifty were from Baltimore secondary schools.

International Exchange—From February 16 to March 1, 1950, 200 posters and pictures made in art classes by junior and senior high pupils for the Junior Red Cross for exchange abroad were shown in eight corridor display cases of the Enoch Pratt Free Library. In 1949 the Baltimore schools contributed 500 paintings to this project. Hundreds of accepted pictures were sent by the American Red Cross to Austria, Australia, Belgium, Canada, Czechoslovakia, France, Germany, Greece, Iran, Japan, Poland, Sweden, Venezuela, and Yugoslavia, in exchange for pictures produced in those countries.

In response to requests for children's paintings received from two overseas countries, nine were sent to Luxembourg, and thirteen to London, England.

The Division of Art Education was also recipient as well as donor. Early in May, 1949, through the Junior Red Cross, a group of seven pictures arrived from Caracas, Venezuela, through the International Art Exchange. The following year a gift of fifteen pictures was received from the Swedish Junior Red Cross in return for pictures made by students of the Eastern High School.

Local Exhibits—The most extensive exhibition of high school art work yet attempted by the Baltimore public schools was shown in the new Saidie A. May Young People's Art Center at the Baltimore Museum of Art from June 4 to June 23, 1950. It included ninety pieces of ceramic sculpture, flat work, handcraft, and architectural models. The exhibition was the cause of favorable comment from the representatives of the Baltimore Museum of Art and from the press.

From February 18 to March 4, 1950 the various processes employed in the art education program of the public secondary schools were exhibited in one of the large show windows of a downtown department store. Students working under the direction of their teachers demonstrated silk-screen printing, pottery, textiles and weaving, painting and sculpture, handcraft and oil painting, paper pulp and paper sculpture, textile decoration and hooked rugs, cartooning, and figure sketching.

For the Mayor's Clean-Up campaign ten secondary schools participated. One hundred of the posters submitted in the project were exhibited at the Peale Museum from May 14 to 26, 1950.

Over one hundred drawings were submitted by four city high schools in the Pratt Library's contest for illustrations for its vacation reading lists. Not only was such a large number of entries gratifying, but the quality of the drawings submitted was remarkable. The winning cover design and illustrations were chosen for originality of idea and appropriateness to purpose as well as good execution. The winners were presented with a gift book or book discount certificates, their original drawings being shown in one of the library's large display windows on Cathedral Street from May 23 through June 13, 1950.

Driver Education

Driver education was initiated in 1946 and extended to include behind-the-wheel training in three schools in February, 1948. By the end of June, 1950, there were eight driver education cars used by eleven secondary schools and one veteran's trade school. The total number of students enrolled was 541.

The original three cars for behind-the-wheel instruction were provided directly by the Automobile Trade Association of Maryland. Two additional cars were secured through the Automobile Club of Maryland, and the other three cars were obtained from dealers through a pool set up by the trade association.

All driver education cars are titled in the name of the Mayor and City Council of Baltimore, Department of Education. The cars, which remain the property of the original owners and are replaced periodically, are assigned to the

THE EVENING CENTERS, SUCH AS THE ONE AT THE BALTIMORE POLYTECHNI
INSTITUTE PROVIDES ADVANCED TRAINING IN OCCUPATIONAL SKILLS AS WELL A
INITIAL TRAINING FOR VARIOUS OCCUPATIONS AND FOR DEVELOPING CIVIC AN
AVOCATIONAL INTERESTS

Department of Education for instructional purposes. The Department of Education assumes full responsibility for garaging, servicing and maintenance of the cars while they are used in the program.

The Department carries maximum insurance ($300,000 per individual or accident) for bodily injury. Adequate insurance ($5,000) is also carried against property damage. The insurance policies cover $1,000 medical payments for each occupant of the car. The Department assumes full responsibility for the condition of the driver education cars and in this area has found it advisable to be self-insurer.

During the current two-year period progress was made in refining the content and method of instruction. In general there was much satisfaction concerning the development of the program. An objective study by the Automobile Club of Maryland (AAA) showed that those who took the Department's course in driver education had fewer accidents than those in comparable age groups that had not had such instruction. One insurance company recognized this influencing factor by declaring lower rates for those boys and girls who had successfully completed the Baltimore driver education course.

Yet by June, 1950, many problems remained: first, extension of the course to include more students during the regular year and during the summer months; second, extension to include driver education at the adult level.

The Department recognized the need for more assistance and guidance in driver education. In the early years of the program the Curriculum Bureau and the Business Office carried the major load. In June, 1950, a Specialist in Safety was appointed to take office in September of that year. Among his duties were to be the administrative aspects of driver education.

Vocational Education

In developing its various courses, the Division of Vocational Education makes extensive use of the generous counsel of business and industrial groups and the technical advisory committees for the various trades and processes taught in the vocational schools. The committees representing business education and distributive education

TABLE 25

CHARACTERISTICS OF DISTRIBUTIVE EDUCATION PROGRAM

Item	1948-49	1949-50
Enrollment of Students	3,211	4,694
Youth, full time (cooperative)	150	182
Adult, part time (day extension)	741	1,057
Adult, part time (evening)	2,320	3,455
Cooperating Employers	61	76
Training hours for adults (day)	13,772	18,534
Business ethics	656	480
Design	600	198
Elevator operator	....	462
Fabrics	1,830	416
Food handling	1,808	3,950
Handwriting	60	550
How to interview	608	....
Human relations	384	2,240
Pre-Christmas training	2,382	1,904
Retail selling	4,490	6,768
Supervisory training	650	792
Telephone technique	....	576
Wrapper training	304	198

were very active throughout the two-year period, especially in the work-study and cooperative programs. The National Office Management Association continued to be very helpful in the training of office employees. The trade advisory committees contributed extensively to the planning of the new Edison-Barton-Mergenthaler vocational high school. The special committees of the baking and foundry trades were called upon to engage in pioneer planning, since the introduction of these two new departments required fundamental decisions as to equipment and layout. Committees of principals, teachers, and supervisors were also of great assistance to the architects and engineers in planning the two new vocational schools and their equipment.

Distributive Education—Vocational education, however, is not confined to the so-called vocational schools. During the biennium there has been continued development of vocational-technical courses in the Baltimore Junior College, the most recent being the outlining of a course in printing for offering in 1950-51. Many of the curricula in the senior high schools are vocational in character and objective, especially the art curriculum, the music curriculum, the business curriculum, and the curriculum in distributive education. This last is concerned with the training of individuals for service in selling. It provides twelfth grade morning instruction in eight senior high schools and afternoon store experience under the supervision of a teacher-coordinator.

The morning instruction deals with selling techniques, merchandise information, fashion, advertising, display,. store arithmetic, and employer-employee relations. Each school has its classroom laboratory, equipped as a store unit with live merchandise for instruction in a realistic setting and for practice.

For one full year the students spend a minimum of fifteen hours each week in school and fifteen hours in a Baltimore store. The classroom anticipates and reviews the problems met in the store. The store work applies the precepts taught in the classroom. The teacher visits the students at the store, watches them work, and discusses training problems with the students' supervisor. Conversely, store executives visit the classroom and give talks about the most recent developments in retailing. Thus, theory and practice are unceasingly interwoven. During this training period the students receive wages, and, upon their high school graduation, offers of continued employment. During 1949-50, 76 Baltimore merchants cooperated in this program.

The program for adults in both day and evening classes developed originally out of the requests of business for assistance in employee training. Courses in human relations, leadership techniques, how to supervise, how to interview, customer relations, and salesmanship have been in continuous demand. Of especial significance for the health of Baltimoreans were the short intensive courses for food handlers operated during the biennium in cooperation with the Baltimore City Department of Health. The health department food handling inspectors organized the classes and the Department of Education provided the instruction. Enrollment ranged from 25 to 200 per class. Large chain organizations in the drug and food business also called for similar courses not only for their employees but for their supervisors and managers as well.

Apprenticeship Training—On April 20, 1950, at graduation exercises for electrical apprentices from the International Brotherhood of Electrical Workers, Local Union Number 28, 95 young men received certificates showing completion of a four-year apprenticeship and the required 576 hours of related instruction (144 hours per year). There were 158 others who received certificates showing the completion of one year of related instruction in connection with their apprenticeships. The courses completed by these men had been developed by the Vocational Division in close cooperation with the Joint Apprenticeship Committee of nine local unions. The total program in each trade was designed to cover three, four, or five years of related instruction and background theory to enable apprentices to qualify as journeymen. During 1949-50 classes were operated in the nine trades indicated in Table 26, with 767 students enrolled. Of the 32 classes organized, all but seven were for related instruction for apprentices in the trades indicated. The exceptions were five classes in electrical code, and two classes in the printing field. The purpose of the electrical code classes was to prepare men who had worked for four or more years in the electrical trades to take examinations to qualify as journeymen electricians or for a Master Electrician's License as required by State laws and local ordinances. The purpose of the two classes in the printing field was to give instructions in advanced selling techniques for printing industry salesmen and modern methods of estimating printing costs.

For veterans who had been accepted as apprentices, a four-year program was set up in thirteen different trade areas. The number of classes, students, and their distribution among the trades are shown in Table 27.

Training Program for Veterans — Under arrangement with the Veterans Administration vocational training for

TABLE 26

RELATED INSTRUCTION CLASSES OPERATED UNDER GEORGE-BARDEN ACT
JULY, 1949—JUNE, 1950

Trade	Number of Classes	Number of Apprentices Enrolled
TOTAL:	32	767
Bricklaying	2	58
Carpentry	5	143
Electric Code	5	140
Electricity	12	253
Plumbing	3	66
Printers	2	64
Automatic Sprinkler	1	19
Auto Mechanics	1	12
Pattern Makers and Foundrymen	1	12

veterans has been supplied by the Department of Education since October, 1945. The program is supported by tuition of $35 per month per student enrolled paid by the United States government. As of June 30, 1950, there were enrolled 277 white and 626 colored veterans, a total of 903. In all, more than 5,100 veterans have enrolled for full-time and half-time trade training courses during the operation of the veterans vocational program.

The local trade and industrial groups have been cooperative to the very limit of their facilities. The actual beginning of this program and its successful operation to date are largely the result of the help received from this source. They contributed key men as instructors and other personnel from their own membership, supplies, and such items as refrigerators, oil burners, electric motors, bricks,

TABLE 27

RELATED INSTRUCTION CLASSES FOR VETERAN APPRENTICES
JULY, 1949—JUNE, 1950

Trade	Number of Classes	Number of Apprentices Enrolled
TOTAL:	53	1,182
White:		
Auto Mechanics	5	131
Auto Body and Fender Mechanics....	2	41
Cabinet Making	2	39
Carpentry	2	59
Electricians	5	121
Floor Coverers	2	27
Machinists	8	154
Plumbers	10	221
Printing	10	248
Pattern Making and Foundrymen....	1	8
Sheet Metal Mechanics	2	28
Sign Painters	1	10
Upholsterers	1	47
Colored:		
Printing	1	26
Supervised Group Study	1	22

wire, and metal. They established a very efficient, cooperative, on-the-job training program for advanced trainees of the veterans' trade schools, whereby selected trainees spent two weeks on the job and then returned to school for two weeks. The local newspapers generously gave publicity to the training programs and new opportunities available for veterans, and the general information so necessary for maintaining an informed public. Special appreciation is also due WMAR-TV of the Baltimore *Sun* for the series of programs which it presented so enthusiastically and effectively to its viewers.

V

STATISTICAL TABLES

TABLE 28

ENROLLMENT OF PUPILS IN DAY SCHOOLS FOR THE SCHOOL YEAR

Type of School	1948-1949 Net Enrollment	1948-1949 Average Net Roll	1949-1950 Net Enrollment	1949-1950 Average Net Roll	Number of Buildings[1]
ALL DAY SCHOOLS[2]	**120,667**	**111,310**	**124,649**	**114,371**	**173**
Full-time Day	120,291	111,100	124,259	114,195	173
Senior High	13,110	12,539	13,663	13,051	9
Vocational High	1,604	1,499	1,745	1,563	6
General Vocational..	1,150	1,107	1,511	1,434	7
Junior High[3]	20,111	19,287	20,574	19,695	18
Occupational	1,837	1,707	1,829	1,711	5
Elementary[4]	81,875	74,462	84,156	76,580	128
Teachers College	181	174	203	195	....
Junior College	423	324	578	445	......
Full-time, White	**80,456**	**74,001**	**82,497**	**75,076**	**107**
Senior High	10,600	10,110	10,955	10,455	8
Vocational High	978	894	1,134	974	3
General Vocational..	723	658	774	738	3
Junior High[3]	14,345	13,687	14,411	13,654	13
Occupational	1,094	1,032	1,110	1,044	4
Elementary[4]	52,293	47,295	53,535	48,146	76
Junior College	423	324	578	445	......
Full-time, Colored ..	**39,835**	**37,099**	**41,762**	**39,119**	**66**
Senior High	2,510	2,429	2,708	2,596	1
Vocational High	626	605	611	589	3
General Vocational..	427	449	737	696	4
Junior High[3]	5,766	5,600	6,163	6,041	5
Occupational	743	675	719	667	1
Elementary[4]	29,582	27,167	30,621	28,434	52
Teachers College	181	174	203	195	......
Part-time Day	**376**	**210**	**390**	**176**	......
Home Instructed:					
White	109	74	113	69	......
Colored	47	46	26	23	......
Hospital Schools:					
White	179	72	214	64	......
Colored	41	18	37	20	......

[1] As of June 1950. Separate building units exclusive of those used for administrative or storage purposes and the hospital schools. Buildings housing schools of different types are shown under the type which uses more than half of the space.

[2] Junior College included.

[3] Includes special classes.

[4] Includes prekindergarten, kindergarten, and special classes but not hospital schools.

TABLE 29

NET ROLL BY GRADES, OCTOBER OF EACH YEAR, 1930 THROUGH 1949

ALL SCHOOLS

Year	Pre-kinder-garten	Kinder-garten	Grades 1-6	Special Schools and Classes	Occupa-tional	Total El'm'ry	Grades 7 and 8	Grades 9-12	Voca-tional	Total Secondary	Colleges*	Total Net Roll*
1930	....	5,384	70,215	2,645	825	79,069	15,925	16,260	1,096	33,281	137	112,487
1931	....	5,313	70,357	2,882	949	79,501	16,093	17,869	1,337	35,299	117	4,917
1932	....	5,587	69,622	3,779	938	79,926	16,734	19,805	1,530	38,069	94	118,089
1933	....	5,359	69,145	4,431	1,854	80,789	16,600	19,783	1,617	38,000	108	118,897
1934	....	4,969	69,024	4,937	2,670	81,600	15,922	20,436	1,800	38,158	110	119,868
1935	....	5,210	67,282	5,774	2,858	81,124	15,575	20,827	2,026	38,428	140	119,692
1936	....	5,004	65,452	6,243	2,793	79,492	15,605	20,467	2,085	38,157	161	117,810
1937	....	5,031	64,126	6,364	2,655	78,176	15,328	20,502	2,064	37,894	164	116,234
1938	55	5,263	61,717	6,757	2,900	76,692	15,456	21,775	2,434	39,665	156	116,513
1939	59	5,456	59,540	6,545	2,939	74,539	15,753	22,287	2,459	40,499	141	115,179
1940	61	5,515	58,079	6,675	3,158	73,488	15,556	22,247	2,464	40,267	156	113,911
1941	60	5,206	58,618	6,309	2,811	73,004	14,753	20,534	2,247	37,534	181	110,719
1942	59	5,501	59,992	5,826	2,416	73,794	14,224	19,122	2,088	35,434	154	109,382
1943	60	5,799	61,334	5,349	2,084	74,626	14,116	17,780	1,923	33,819	128	108,573
1944	60	5,462	60,727	5,446	1,867	73,562	13,846	17,740	1,967	33,553	134	107,249
1945	88	5,607	58,656	5,502	1,939	71,792	13,149	17,799	2,272	33,220	123	105,135
1946	90	6,362	58,212	5,420	1,789	71,873	13,125	18,107	2,779	34,011	125	106,009
1947	90	7,616	58,966	5,103	1,841	73,616	13,211	18,354	2,780	34,345	318	108,279
1948	90	8,642	61,623	4,644	1,713	76,712	13,673	18,453	2,598	34,724	468	1,904
1949	120	8,149	64,459	4,543	1,722	78,993	13,997	19,120	3,074	36,191	629	115,813

*Includes Baltimore Junior College and Coppin Teachers College.

TABLE 30

Net Roll by Grades, October of Each Year, 1930 through 1949

White

Year	Pre-kindergarten	Kindergarten	Grades 1-6	Special Schools and Classes	Occupational	Total Elementary	Grades 7 and 8	Grades 9-12	Vocational	Total Secondary	Junior College	Total Net Roll
1930	......	4,327	53,991	2,335	656	61,309	13,564	13,971	818	28,353	......	89,662
1931	......	4,238	53,139	2,573	720	60,670	13,695	15,475	988	30,158	......	90,828
1932	......	4,479	51,811	3,057	698	60,045	14,199	17,170	1,116	32,485	......	92,530
1933	......	4,230	50,848	3,460	1,235	59,773	13,984	17,226	1,155	32,365	......	92,138
1934	......	3,929	49,869	3,889	2,066	59,753	13,364	17,781	1,288	32,433	......	92,186
1935	......	4,049	48,150	4,377	2,277	58,853	12,916	18,157	1,513	32,586	......	91,439
1936	......	3,803	46,221	4,688	2,191	56,903	12,773	17,734	1,586	32,093	......	88,996
1937	......	3,773	44,574	4,663	2,021	55,031	12,449	17,606	1,585	31,640	......	86,671
1938	55	3,894	42,754	4,478	2,129	53,310	12,261	18,625	1,855	32,741	......	86,051
1939	59	4,009	40,595	4,207	2,116	50,986	12,367	18,871	1,905	33,143	......	84,129
1940	61	4,012	39,256	3,943	2,198	49,470	12,077	18,691	2,043	32,811	......	82,281
1941	60	3,896	39,274	3,637	1,953	48,820	11,377	17,238	1,812	30,427	......	79,247
1942	59	4,091	40,244	3,411	1,630	49,435	10,944	16,078	1,617	28,639	......	78,074
1943	60	4,246	41,332	3,180	1,273	50,091	10,800	14,908	1,487	27,195	......	77,286
1944	60	3,909	40,195	3,008	1,165	48,337	10,412	14,651	1,455	26,518	......	74,855
1945	58	4,060	37,927	2,968	1,194	46,207	9,716	14,563	1,514	25,793	......	72,000
1946	60	4,579	37,130	2,918	1,140	45,827	9,446	14,659	1,671	25,776	......	71,603
1947	60	5,480	37,275	2,728	1,095	46,638	9,464	14,574	1,611	25,649	154	72,441
1948	60	6,2	38,859	2,457	1,002	48,600	9,551	14,504	1,575	25,630	291	74,521
1949	60	5,499	40,558	2,373	1,040	49,530	9,592	14,875	1,776	26,243	430	76,203

TABLE 31

Net Roll by Grades, October of Each Year, 1930 Through 1949

Colored

Year	Pre-kindergarten	Kindergarten	Grades 1-6	Special Schools and Classes	Occupational	Total Elementary	Grades 7 and 8	Grades 9-12	Vocational	Total Secondary	Teachers College	Total Net Roll
1930	....	1,67	16,24	310	169	17,60	2,361	2,289	28	4,98	137	22,85
1931	....	1,05	17,28	309	229	18,81	2,398	2,394	39	5,41	117	24,89
1932	....	1,108	17,81	722	240	19,81	2,535	2,635	44	5,84	94	25,59
1933	....	1,29	18,97	971	619	21,06	2,616	2,557	62	5,85	108	26,59
1934	....	1,040	19,55	1,048	604	21,87	2,558	2,655	52	5,25	110	27,82
1935	....	1,61	19,32	1,397	581	22,21	2,659	2,670	53	5,82	140	28,83
1936	....	1,201	19,231	1,555	602	22,89	2,832	2,733	89	6,04	161	28,84
1937	....	1,38	19,52	1,701	634	23,45	2,879	2,896	79	6,84	164	29,63
1938	....	1,89	18,63	2,279	771	23,82	3,195	3,50	59	6,84	156	30,62
1939	....	1,447	18,85	2,338	823	23,53	3,386	3,46	54	7,86	141	31,60
1940	....	1,63	18,83	2,732	960	24,08	3,479	3,56	31	7,86	156	31,80
1941	....	1,30	19,84	2,672	858	24,84	3,376	3,96	35	7,07	181	31,42
1942	....	1,40	19,78	2,415	786	24,89	3,280	3,94	471	6,95	154	31,08
1943	....	1,53	20,02	2,169	811	24,535	3,316	2,872	86	6,84	128	31,287
1944	....	1,53	20,32	2,438	702	25,225	3,434	3,089	52	7,85	134	32,94
1945	30	1,547	20,29	2,534	745	25,585	3,433	3,236	58	7,87	123	33,85
1946	30	1,83	21,82	2,502	649	26,046	3,679	3,448	1,108	8,85	125	34,06
1947	30	2,36	21,81	2,375	746	26,978	3,747	3,780	1,169	8,86	164	35,88
1948	30	2,80	22,64	2,187	711	28,112	4,122	3,949	1,023	9,04	177	37,83
1949	60	2,60	23,81	2,170	682	29,463	4,405	4,245	1,298	9,88	199	39,610

TABLE 32

AVERAGE DAILY ATTENDANCE IN FULL-TIME DAY SCHOOLS [1]

Type of School	1948-1949 Average Attendance	Per Cent	1949-1950 Average Attendance	Per Cent
FULL-TIME DAY SCHOOLS [1]	99,358	90.3	103,785	89.6
Senior High	11,474	91.4	12,287	92.5
Vocational High	1,339	89.3	1,459	90.3
General Vocational	962	86.9	1,198	84.6
Junior High	17,636	91.4	18,177	92.6
Occupational	1,395	81.7	1,369	76.6
Elementary	66,075	88.7	68,689	91.7
Teachers College	172	98.8	189	95.0
Baltimore Junior College	305	94.1	417	93.8
Total White Schools	66,377	90.0	68,608	89.8
Senior High	9,218	91.9	9,863	92.6
Vocational High	823	92.0	945	92.0
General Vocational	582	88.4	633	88.0
Junior High	12,594	92.0	12,728	93.2
Occupational	858	83.1	842	76.8
Elementary	41,997	88.7	43,180	92.5
Baltimore Junior College	305	94.1	417	93.8
Total Colored Schools	32,981	87.5	35,177	87.6
Senior High	2,256	92.8	2,424	92.1
Vocational High	516	85.1	514	87.6
General Vocational	380	84.6	565	81.0
Junior High	5,042	90.0	5,449	91.1
Occupational	537	79.5	527	76.4
Elementary	24,078	81.6	25,509	90.3
Teachers College	172	98.8	189	95.0

[1] Includes Baltimore Junior College.

Number of Sessions	1948-49	1949-50
Elementary-Secondary	188	184
Baltimore Junior College	170	162

TABLE 33

ENROLLMENT AND ATTENDANCE IN KINDERGARTENS AND PRE-
KINDERGARTENS FOR THE YEAR ENDING JUNE 30TH

Year	No.*	Enrollment	June Net Roll	Average Net Roll	Average Attend.	Per Cent Attend.
KINDERGARTENS—						
Total:						
1950............	87	11,354	7,155	7,581	6,486	86.1
1949............	87	11,895	7,185	7,843	6,522	84.4
White:						
1950............	67	7,784	4,859	5,185	4,368	84.1
1949............	67	8,463	4,945	5,585	4,518	80.1
Colored:						
1950............	20	3,570	2,296	2,396	2,118	88.1
1949............	20	3,432	2,240	2,258	2,004	88.7
PREKINDERGARTENS—						
Total:						
1950............	4	162	120	120	99	84.1
1949............	3	117	92	88	75	87.7
White:						
1950............	2	87	60	60	49	81.3
1949............	2	78	62	58	47	81.1
Colored:						
1950............	2	75	60	60	50	87.0
1949............	1	39	30	30	28	93.0

Schools having morning and afternoon sessions:

Year	Total	White	Colored
1950............................	83	64	19
1949............................	82	62	20

Pupils advanced from kindergartens to first grade:

Year	Total	White	Colored
1950............................	5,330	3,551	1,779
1949............................	5,122	3,489	1,633

* Number of schools having a kindergarten or a prekindergarten.

TABLE 34
ENROLLMENT AND ATTENDANCE IN CLASSES FOR THE PHYSICALLY HANDICAPPED

Year	No.*	Enrollment	June Net Roll	Average Net Roll	Average Attend.	Per Cent Attend.
TOTAL ALL SCHOOLS:						
1950...........	32	574	528	528	469	87.6
1949...........	32	585	522	518	463	89.3
Orthopedic:						
1950...........	15	330	296	295	259	88.0
1949...........	15	318	281	277	248	89.5
All Others:						
1950...........	17	244	232	233	210	87.5
1949...........	17	267	241	241	215	89.2
WHITE TOTAL:						
1950...........	22	409	377	380	340	89.2
1949...........	22	435	382	378	341	90.2
Orthopedic:						
1950...........	10	235	214	214	188	88.0
1949...........	10	236	209	204	184	90.1
Sight Cons.:						
1950...........	3	46	43	43	38	88.4
1949...........	3	50	46	47	40	85.1
Hear. Cons.:						
1950...........	4	41	35	36	34	91.0
1949...........	3	40	39	40	38	95.0
Deaf:						
1950...........	3	29	29	30	28	89.0
1949...........	3	46	30	30	27	90.0
Mixed: [1]						
1950...........	2	58	56	57	52	90.0
1949...........	3	63	58	57	52	91.2
COLORED TOTAL:						
1950...........	10	165	151	148	129	85.5
1949...........	10	150	140	140	122	87.1
Orthopedic:						
1950...........	5	95	82	81	71	88.0
1949...........	5	82	72	73	64	87.6
Sight Cons.:						
1950...........	3	49	48	47	41	88.0
1949...........	3	46	46	44	41	93.1
Hear. Cons.:						
1950...........	1	13	13	12	10	84.0
1949...........	1	13	12	10	7	70.0
Deaf:						
1950...........	1	8	8	8	7	82.0
1949...........	1	9	10	13	10	76.9

*Number of classes.
[1] Junior high class consisting of pupils with the following deficiencies:

	Orthopedic	Sight Cons.	Hear.	Deaf	Cardiac
1950	34	7	3	3	11
1949	26	7	4	4	15

TABLE 35

ENROLLMENT AND ATTENDANCE IN CLASSES FOR THE MENTALLY HANDICAPPED

Year	No.*	Enrollment	June Net Roll	Average Net Roll	Average Attend.	Per Cent Attend.
TOTAL ALL SCHOOLS:						
1950............	204	4,573	3,898	3,935	3,159	81.4
1949............	197	5,182	3,854	4,021	3,184	79.1
Opportunity:						
1950............	128	2,632	2,341	2,313	1,926	83.8
1949............	120	3,169	2,368	2,487	2,027	75.7
Special Center:						
1950............	1	18	17	17	14	80.0
1949............	3	83	56	55	44	80.0
Shop Center:						
1950............	75	1,923	1,540	1,605	1,219	79.6
1949............	74	1,930	1,430	1,479	1,113	75.2
WHITE TOTAL:						
1950............	101	2,339	1,957	2,127	1,709	80.1
1949............	96	2,571	1,848	2,036	1,637	80.4
Opportunity:						
1950............	65	1,342	1,190	1,327	1,121	84.5
1949............	63	1,634	1,203	1,346	1,123	83.4
Special Center:						
1950............	1	18	17	17	14	80.0
1949............	1	20	19	19	16	84.2
Shop Center:						
1950............	35	979	750	783	574	76.8
1949............	32	917	626	671	498	74.2
COLORED TOTAL:						
1950............	103	2,234	1,941	1,808	1,450	82.7
1949............	101	2,611	2,006	1,985	1,547	77.9
Opportunity:						
1950............	63	1,290	1,151	986	805	83.1
1949............	57	1,535	1,165	1,141	904	79.2
Special Center:						
1950............	....	......	......	......	......	......
1949............	2	63	37	36	28	77.7
Shop Center:						
1950............	40	944	790	822	645	82.4
1949............	42	1,013	804	808	615	76.1

* Number of classes.

TABLE 36
EDUCATION PROGRAMS FOR ADULTS

Program	Total	1948-1949 White	Colored	Total	1949-1950 White	Colored
ENROLLMENT						
All year	24,369	17,708	6,661	26,984	20,538	6,446
Summer Only	1,665	989	676	1,143	766	377
Fall-winter-spring [1]	22,704	16,719	5,985	25,841	19,772	6,069
AVERAGE NET ROLL	13,030	8,287	4,743	13,734	9,342	4,392
Americanization	582	582	......	802	802	......
Academic—Elementary	761	127	634	743	133	610
Junior High	359	119	240	330	146	184
Secondary	2,708	1,982	726	2,849	1,964	885
Vocational—Veterans	2,073	1,144	929	1,930	944	986
Apprenticeship	299	299	......	425	425	......
Distributive Education	552	552	......	274	274	......
Smith-Hughes	858	511	347	910	608	302
Home Economics	1,643	448	1,195	1,382	456	926
Indust. Non-Smith-Hughes	213	168	45	223	195	28
Non-Credit	889	869	20	1,889	1,875	14
Parent Education	1,904	1,388	516	1,977	1,520	457
Veterans Institute	189	98	91	......	......	......
AVERAGE ATTENDANCE	9,798	6,304	3,494	10,292	7,066	3,226
Americanization	422	422	......	584	584	......
Academic—Elementary	550	95	455	391	96	295
Junior High	270	94	176	263	118	145
Secondary	2,063	1,538	525	2,234	1,559	675
Vocational—Veterans	1,684	892	792	1,577	742	835
Apprenticeship	239	239	......	376	376	......
Distributive Education	509	509	......	242	242	......
Smith-Hughes	662	377	285	677	444	233
Home Economics	1,073	317	756	1,007	327	680
Indust. Non-Smith-Hughes	163	128	35	164	144	20
Non-Credit	619	604	15	1,291	1,280	11
Parent Education	1,390	1,013	377	1,486	1,154	332
Veterans Institute	154	76	78	......	......	......
TOTAL FACULTY (Feb.)	477	351	126	506	366	140

CLASS MEETINGS:	Number	Number
Americanization-Elementary-Secondary	89	91
Smith-Hughes Vocational	61	61
Accelerate High School	133	130
Parent Education	89	89

[1] Includes programs beginning July 1 and continuing throughout the year.

TABLE 37

PERMANENT WITHDRAWALS FROM FULL-TIME DAY SCHOOLS (EXCLUDING GRADUATES) 1948-49

Cause	All Day Schools¹ No.	%	Total White No.	%	White Senior High No.	%	White Vocational No.	%	White Junior High No.	%	White Occupational No.	%	White Elementary No.	%
ALL	8976	....	6505	....	995	....	585	....	1118	....	354	....	3453	....
Farm or home employment	613	6.8	448	7.4	63	6.3	80	13.7	263	23.5	23	6.5	19	.6
Removal from city	3490	38.9	2724	41.8	122	12.3	40	6.8	395	35.3	39	11.0	2128	61.6
Physical disability	841	9.4	432	6.6	46	4.6	19	3.2	57	5.1	9	2.5	301	8.7
Local on-public schools	340	3.8	319	4.9	18	1.9	4	.7	50	4.5	5	1.5	242	7.0
Under age	503	5.6	443	6.8	....	....	....	....	....	....	....	....	443	12.8
Work permit	576	6.4	502	7.7	237	23.8	50	8.5	122	110	46	13.0	47	1.4
Institution	245	2.7	144	2.2	4	.4	27	4.6	22	2.0	26	7.3	65	1.9
Marriage	137	1.5	65	.9	46	4.6	5	.9	8	.7	3	.9	3	.1
Over 16	1989	22.2	1283	19.6	402	40.4	324	55.4	192	17.1	203	57.3	162	4.7
Whereabouts unknown	120	1.3	47	.7	3	.3	....	....	6	.5	....	....	38	1.1
Excluded	41	.5	33	.5	9	.9	19	3.2	....	....	....	....	5	.1
med Forces	81	.9	65	.9	45	4.5	17	3.0	3	.3	....	....	....	....

¹ White and colored full-time day schools exclusive of Coppin Teachers College.

Senior High School Diplomas..... 2,822
Vocational School Diplomas...... 894

TABLE 38

PERMANENT WITHDRAWALS FROM FULL-TIME DAY SCHOOLS (EXCLUDING GRADUATES) 1949-50

Cause	All Day Schools¹ No.	%	Total White No.	%	White Senior High No.	%	White Vocational No.	%	White Junior High No.	%	White Occupational No.	%	White Elementary No.	%
TOTAL	8377	....	6095	....	967	....	550	....	891	....	313	....	3374	....
Farm or home employment	133	1.3	63	1.0	40	4.1	12	2.2	7	.8	1	.3	3	.1
Removal from city	3520	42.0	2886	47.4	152	15.7	53	9.6	417	46.8	33	10.5	2231	66.1
Physical disability	796	9.6	408	6.7	67	6.9	23	4.2	79	8.9	24	7.7	215	6.4
Local non-public schools	381	4.5	360	6.0	24	2.5	5	.9	69	7.7	7	2.3	255	7.6
Under age	421	5.0	352	5.8	...	...	...	...	...	...	...	...	352	10.4
Work permit	230	2.7	211	3.4	149	15.4	22	4.0	24	2.7	5	1.6	11	.3
Truancy	295	3.5	183	3.0	4	.4	20	3.6	41	4.6	29	9.3	89	2.6
Marriage	176	2.1	114	1.8	60	6.2	20	3.6	18	2.0	4	1.3	12	.4
Over 16	2213	26.4	1381	22.6	409	42.4	380	69.1	228	25.6	207	66.1	157	4.7
...ts unknown	169	2.0	84	1.4	31	3.2	6	1.1	5	.6	2	.6	40	1.2
Excluded	30	.4	24	.4	6	.6	6	1.1	2	.2	1	.3	9	.2
Armed Forces	33	.5	29	.5	25	2.6	3	.6	1	.1	...	...	...	...

¹ White and colored full-time day schools exclusive of Coppin Teachers College.

Senior high school diplomas...... 3,667

Vocational school diplomas...... 345

TABLE 39

PERMANENT WITHDRAWALS FROM FULL-TIME DAY SCHOOLS (EXCLUDING GRADUATES) 1948-49

Cause	Total Colored¹ No.	%	Colored Senior High No.	%	Colored Vocational No.	%	Colored Junior High No.	%	Colored Occupational No.	%	Colored Elementary No.	%	Coppin Teachers College No.	%
TOTAL	2471	....	274	....	335	....	514	....	163	....	1185	....	9	....
Farm or home employment	165	6.7	27	9.8	63	18.8	67	13.0	6	3.7	2	.2	...	....
Removal farm city	766	31.0	23	8.4	29	8.7	88	17.1	20	12.3	606	51.1	1	11.1
Physical disability	409	16.6	36	13.1	29	8.7	123	24.0	24	14.7	197	16.6	2	22.2
Local public schools	21	.8	1	.4	...	....	2	.4	1	.6	17	1.4	...	....
Under age	60	2.4	...	....	...	....	...	....	...	....	60	5.1	...	....
Work permit	74	3.0	5	1.8	9	2.7	37	7.2	20	12.3	3	.3	...	....
Institution	101	4.1	1	.4	6	1.8	17	3.3	10	6.1	67	5.7	1	11.1
Marriage	72	2.9	36	13.1	16	4.7	16	3.1	1	.6	3	.3	2	22.2
Over 16	706	28.6	133	48.5	176	52.5	142	27.6	74	45.4	181	15.2	2	22.2
Whereabouts unknown	73	3.0	5	1.8	...	....	17	3.3	6	3.7	45	3.8	...	....
Excluded	8	.3	1	.4	...	....	2	.4	1	.6	4	.3	1	11.2
Armed Forces	16	.6	6	2.3	7	2.1	3	.6	...	....	...	....	...	....

¹ Exclusive of Coppin Teachers College.

Senior high school diplomas.......... 569
Vocational school diplomas......... 147
Degrees: Coppin Teachers College 20

TABLE 40

PERMANENT WITHDRAWALS FROM FULL-TIME DAY SCHOOLS (EXCLUDING GRADUATES) 1949-50

Cause	Total Colored[1] No.	%	Colored Senior High No.	%	Colored Vocational No.	%	Colored Junior High No.	%	Colored Occupational No.	%	Colored Elementary No.	%	Coppin Teachers College No.	%
TOTAL	2282	.....	252	.....	368	.....	446	.....	168	.....	1048	.....	11	.....
Farm or home employment	50	2.2	17	6.7	27	7.3	3	.7	1	.6	2	.2	...	...
Removal from city	634	27.8	15	6.0	18	4.9	101	22.7	14	8.3	486	46.3	1	9.1
Physical disability	388	17.0	38	15.1	40	10.9	102	22.9	16	9.6	192	18.3	8	72.7
Col. non-public schools	21	.9	...	...	...	...	...	...	1	.6	20	1.9	...	...
Under age	69	3.0	...	...	...	...	...	...	...	...	69	6.6	...	...
Wk permit	19	.8	3	1.2	6	1.6	9	2.0	...	...	1	.1	...	...
Institution	112	4.9	4	1.6	2	.6	22	4.9	16	9.6	68	6.5	1	9.1
Marriage	62	2.7	22	8.7	10	2.7	16	3.6	1	.6	13	1.2	1	9.1
Over 16	832	36.5	144	57.1	243	66.0	182	40.8	117	69.6	46	14.0	...	...
Abts unknown	85	3.7	7	2.8	20	5.4	9	2.0	2	1.1	47	4.5	...	...
Excluded	6	.3	...	...	...	...	2	.4	...	...	4	.4	...	...
Armed Forces	4	.2	2	.8	2	.6	...	...	...	...	...	...	...	...

[1] Exclusive of Coppin Teachers College.

Senior high school diplomas............. 1,283
Vocational school diplomas............. 254
Degrees: Coppin Teachers College...... 31

TABLE 41
PER CENT OF NET ROLL PROMOTED[1] AS OF JANUARY 1948, 1949, AND 1950
WHITE ELEMENTARY SCHOOLS

Number of Promotions	January, 1948 B	G	January, 1949 B	G	January, 1950 B	G
TOTALS—						
Once	94.5	96.7	94.5	92.9	95.5	97.5
Twice	1.1	.9	.3	.4	.3	.3
Grade 1B						
Once	*	*	92.6	91.1	98.3	98.5
Twice	....	....	....	....	....	....
Grade 1A						
Once	93.2	96.8	96.6	91.2	94.0	96.4
Twice	.2	.1	....	.1	....	....
Grade 2B						
Once	*	*	95.1	93.5	98.6	99.3
Twice	....	....	....	....	....	†
Grade 2A						
Once	95.3	97.2	90.7	86.1	89.8	95.6
Twice	.2	.1	....	....	.5	.2
Grade 3B						
Once	95.1	97.1	99.2	96.9	97.2	98.8
Twice	.7	1.0	.6	.7	.6	.5
Grade 3A						
Once	94.1	96.8	93.4	88.0	85.5	93.4
Twice	.1	.4	.2	.3	.2	.4
Grade 4B						
Once	94.4	96.7	99.4	99.5	97.0	98.0
Twice	.9	1.0	.5	.9	.6	.8
Grade 4A						
Once	94.5	95.3	89.3	87.6	93.1	94.7
Twice	1.1	1.5	.2	.1	.3	.2
Grade 5B						
Once	94.7	97.1	93.8	95.7	95.9	96.6
Twice	1.7	1.0	.7	.5	.6	.3
Grade 5A						
Once	93.5	95.8	93.8	90.3	93.9	96.5
Twice	2.3	1.1	.3	.1	.2	.1
Grade 6B						
Once	95.2	95.7	93.6	93.8	96.9	98.5
Twice	1.8	1.4	.5	1.0	.5	.9
Grade 6A						
Once	94.6	96.9	89.8	90.7	97.5	98.2
Twice	2.6	.8	.6	1.0	.1	.3

[1] Based on the number of children on roll at the end of the term—not comparable with rates reported to June, 1932. Exclusive of schools reporting on an annual basis.
* Under "continuous growth" policy no promotional decisions were made at end of first half-year in grades 1 and 2. † Less than .05 per cent.

TABLE 42
PER CENT OF NET ROLL PROMOTED [1] AS OF JUNE 1948, 1949, AND 1950
WHITE ELEMENTARY SCHOOLS

Number of Promotions	June, 1948 B	G	June, 1949 B	G	June, 1950 B	G
TOTALS—						
Once	94.3	96.5	93.5	96.5	93.2	96.4
Twice	.1	.1	.1	.1	†	†
Grade 1B						
Once	*	*	98.2	98.8	96.0	97.9
Twice			....	....	....	....
Grade 1A						
Once	93.9	95.7	92.4	96.2	91.7	95.0
Twice	.1	†	†	†	....	....
Grade 2B						
Once	*	*	95.7	98.4	96.1	98.1
Twice	....	....	....	....	....	....
Grade 2A						
Once	92.5	96.2	91.5	95.7	91.2	96.5
Twice	.1	†	.1	†	.1	.1
Grade 3B						
Once	91.0	94.1	90.6	94.3	93.0	97.4
Twice	.1	.3	.2	.7	....	....
Grade 3A						
Once	92.7	96.1	90.8	94.6	90.0	94.8
Twice	.3	....	.1	....	†	....
Grade 4B						
Once	94.5	96.4	89.0	94.5	93.6	97.0
Twice	.4	.1	.2	.2	.1	....
Grade 4A						
Once	96.0	97.5	93.9	96.6	92.4	95.6
Twice	.1	....	.4	.4	†	.2
Grade 5B						
Once	92.4	95.3	94.1	96.7	93.0	95.6
Twice	.2	.5	.1	.3	.1	....
Grade 5A						
Once	96.5	97.9	95.2	97.5	94.9	97.0
Twice	.2	....	.1	.1	....	.1
Grade 6B						
Once	96.2	96.9	94.7	96.0	94.5	95.4
Twice	.2	....	....	.2	....	....
Grade 6A						
Once	98.0	98.2	96.9	98.2	97.0	97.7
Twice	.2	.1	.1	.1	....	....

[1] Based on the number of children on roll at the end of the term—not comparable with rates reported to June, 1932. Exclusive of schools reporting on an annual basis.
† Less than .05 per cent. * Under "continuous growth" policy no promotional decisions were made at end of first half-year in grades 1 and 2.

TABLE 43
PER CENT OF NET ROLL PROMOTED [1] AS OF JANUARY 1948, 1949, AND 1950
COLORED ELEMENTARY SCHOOLS

Number of Promotions	January, 1948 B	G	January, 1949 B	G	January, 1950 B	G
TOTALS—						
Once	90.2	94.6	89.1	88.8	93.0	96.3
Twice	.6	.7	.3	.4	.3	.3
Grade 1B						
Once	*	*	94.7	93.6	97.2	98.1
Twice	....	....	....	....	....	....
Grade 1A						
Once	91.6	96.5	95.8	90.8	91.1	94.7
Twice	....	....	....	.3	....	....
Grade 2B						
Once	*	*	98.8	95.6	97.2	98.5
Twice	....	....	....	....	....	....
Grade 2A						
Once	91.2	96.0	98.3	90.9	89.8	94.6
Twice	....	....	....	....	.1	.2
Grade 3B						
Once	90.8	96.4	89.0	86.1	94.7	97.4
Twice	.1	.1	.1	.2	.5	.2
Grade 3A						
Once	91.2	95.4	90.2	85.9	85.3	94.3
Twice	.1	.2	.2	.2	....	....
Grade 4B						
Once	87.3	94.0	90.1	94.7	92.9	95.8
Twice	.7	.6	.1	.3	.1	.4
Grade 4A						
Once	91.4	94.9	97.2	99.6	89.8	94.4
Twice	1.4	1.4	.2	.3	.3	....
Grade 5B						
Once	89.1	92.2	79.4	81.8	93.4	97.0
Twice	.9	2.2	.8	.5	.8	1.1
Grade 5A						
Once	91.2	94.6	84.4	87.0	90.0	95.5
Twice	.8	.6	.2	.6	.3	....
Grade 6B						
Once	88.7	93.7	72.8	74.5	93.9	95.5
Twice	1.4	.9	.5	.9	1.0	1.5
Grade 6A						
Once	90.6	93.0	86.8	94.0	92.2	95.3
Twice	1.5	.9	1.4	1.2	.2	.7

[1] Based on the number of children on roll at the end of the term—not comparable with rates reported to June, 1932. Exclusive of schools reporting on an annual basis.
* Under "continuous growth" policy no promotional decisions were made at end of first half-year in grades 1 and 2.

TABLE 44

PER CENT OF NET ROLL PROMOTED [1] AS OF JUNE 1948, 1949, AND 1950
COLORED ELEMENTARY SCHOOLS

Number of Promotions	June, 1948 B	June, 1948 G	June, 1949 B	June, 1949 G	June, 1950 B	June, 1950 C
TOTALS—						
Once	92.1	95.4	90.2	94.6	89.6	95.6
Twice	.1	....	.1	.1	....	....
Grade 1B						
Once	*	*	98.4	99.0	94.9	95.4
Twice			....	....	....	....
Grade 1A						
Once	95.1	96.8	92.1	93.6	92.1	94.9
Twice	....	....	.3	.4	....	....
Grade 2B						
Once	*	*	93.7	97.4	92.4	96.6
Twice			....	....	....	....
Grade 2A						
Once	93.1	96.7	90.5	95.6	88.8	94.3
Twice	.1	....	....	....	....	....
Grade 3B						
Once	89.8	94.3	82.4	92.8	92.3	94.4
Twice	....	....	....	....	....	....
Grade 3A						
Once	91.8	95.9	85.9	93.4	84.6	94.2
Twice	....	....	....	....	....	....
Grade 4B						
Once	88.1	95.3	86.6	92.2	88.1	94.2
Twice	....	....	....	....	....	....
Grade 4A						
Once	91.9	95.7	91.7	94.5	85.3	92.0
Twice	....	....	....	....	....	....
Grade 5B						
Once	91.6	92.3	91.4	94.7	89.0	90.3
Twice	....	....	....	....	....	....
Grade 5A						
Once	92.9	95.0	89.6	95.1	91.0	95.3
Twice	....	....	†	.5	....	....
Grade 6B						
Once	90.3	94.0	92.3	93.5	90.3	93.9
Twice	.1	....	....	....	....	....
Grade 6A						
Once	92.4	95.1	91.3	95.4	91.2	95.7
Twice	....	....	....	....	....	....

[1] Based on the number of children on roll at the end of the term—not comparable with rates reported prior to June, 1932. Exclusive of schools reporting on an annual basis. * Under "continuous growth" policy no promotional decisions are made at end of first half-year in grades 1 and 2. † Less than .05 per cent.

TABLE 45
ACHIEVEMENT BY SUBJECTS—WHITE JUNIOR AND SENIOR HIGH SCHOOLS
SECOND SEMESTER, 1948-49

| Subject | JUNIOR HIGH | | | | SENIOR HIGH | |
	Number Boys	Taking Girls	Per Cent Achieving Boys	Girls	Number Taking	Per Cent Achieving
Algebra	....	....	....	....	1,213	84.3
Analytical Geometry	....	....	....	....	86	79.1
Art	6,526	7,002	99.0	99.7	2,376	97.2
Biology	....	....	....	....	2,997	89.9
Bookkeeping	....	1	....	100.0	1,143	92.4
Business Organization	....	....	....	....	117	97.4
Calculus	....	....	....	....	79	96.2
Chemistry	....	....	....	....	1,577	92.8
Civics	864	913	90.6	93.2	....	....
Commercial Arithmetic	233	1,016	89.3	93.6	....	....
Distributive Education	....	....	....	....	166	100.0
Economics	....	....	....	....	273	98.2
English	6,554	7,039	90.6	96.1	9,966	92.3
French	319	321	94.0	98.4	1,326	92.0
General Science	3,885	3.930	95.0	98.5	....	....
Geography	3,215	3,399	92.6	94.9	819	91.7
German	75	....	100.0	....	629	92.1
History	5,734	6,145	93.5	96.1	6,334	92.8
Home Economics	232	9,578	98.3	98.8	1,900	95.3
Hygiene	2,338	2,502	96.8	98.4	....	....
Industrial Arts	6,856	279	98.4	100.0	2,419	97.1
Junior Business Training	1,470	2,416	97.1	98.8	....	....
Latin	414	478	92.5	96.2	984	94.8
Mathematics	6,496	6,177	90.4	94.6	871	84.5
Mechanical Drawing	3,042	9	97.3	100.0	2,375	94.7
Music	3,546	3,779	99.6	99.8	8,128	99.7
Office Machines	....	....	....	....	117	100.0
Office Practice	....	....	....	....	1,026	96.7
Penmanship	99	142	100.0	100.0	....	....
Physical Education	6,490	6,984	98.8	99.1	9,048	98.2
Physics	....	....	....	....	1,391	88.4
Plane Geometry	....	....	....	....	2,402	83.1
Reading	3,178	3,393	95.4	98.1	....	....
Solid Geometry	....	....	....	....	555	87.2
Spanish	227	86	93.0	98.8	1,604	91.1
Stenography	....	....	....	....	798	95.0
Trigonometry	....	....	....	....	810	84.8
Typing	238	1,315	89.9	94.4	3,127	89.7
Vocations	1,007	1,028	100.0	100.0	....	....

TABLE 46
ACHIEVEMENT BY SUBJECTS—WHITE JUNIOR AND SENIOR HIGH SCHOOLS
SECOND SEMESTER, 1949-50

| Subject | JUNIOR HIGH | | | | SENIOR HIGH | |
| | Number Taking | | Per Cent Achieving | | Number | Per Cent Achieving |
	Boys	Girls	Boys	Girls	Taking	
Algebra	....	....	....	....	1,232	83.2
Analytical Geometry	....	....	....	....	106	89.6
Art	6,735	7,157	99.0	99.5	2,852	98,2
Biology	....	....	....	....	3,205	90.5
Bookkeeping	....	....	....	....	1,411	88.1
Business Organization	....	....	....	....	633	94.0
Calculus	....	....	....	....	77	90.3
Chemistry	....	....	....	....	1,583	95.4
Civics	1,015	926	90.4	94.3	....	....
Commercial Arithmetic	176	740	88.1	94.2	120	90.0
Distributive Education	....	....	....	....	193	98.4
Economics	....	....	....	....	363	96.1
English	6,716	7,150	89.9	96.0	10,583	90.7
French	269	209	97.8	100.0	1,527	93.1
General Science	3,459	3,559	96.2	96.2	....	....
Geography	3,426	3,568	92.2	94.2	1,154	91.3
German	74	....	94.6	....	615	93.7
History	5,725	6,216	93.3	95.5	880	91.5
Home Economics	36	8,390	94.4	98.4	2,137	94.8
Hygiene	2,401	2,639	96.6	98.1	....	....
Industrial Arts	7,109	49	98.1	98.0	2,517	97.1
Junior Business Training	1,253	2,353	95.2	97.7	....	....
Latin	290	482	93.4	97.1	938	93.8
Mathematics	6,603	6,381	89.2	93.1	1,449	90.3
Mechanical Drawing	3,426	11	96.4	100.0	2,339	95.1
Music	3,456	3,880	98.8	99.8	8,526	99.5
Office Machines	....	....	....	....	136	97.8
Office Practice	....	....	....	....	1,017	97.1
Penmanship	148	169	100.0	100.0	....	....
Physical Education	6,684	7,122	98.0	98.4	9,604	98.6
Physics	....	....	....	....	1,300	89.1
Plane Geometry	....	....	....	....	2,211	82.9
Reading	2,794	2,899	95.5	97.2	....	....
Solid Geometry	....	....	....	....	363	90.1
Spanish	337	209	95.3	98.1	1,519	92.8
Stenography	....	....	....	....	902	94.5
Trigonometry	....	....	....	....	864	86.8
Typing	550	1,568	92.4	92.8	4,168	89.0
Vocations	884	885	100.0	100.0	....	....

TABLE 47

ACHIEVEMENTS BY SUBJECTS—COLORED JUNIOR AND
SENIOR HIGH SCHOOLS
SECOND SEMESTER, 1948-49

| | JUNIOR HIGH | | | | SENIOR HIGH | |
| | Number Taking | | Per Cent Achieving | | Number | Per Cent Achiev- |
Subject	Boys	Girls	Boys	Girls	Taking	ing
Algebra	....	....	....	....	113	100.0
Art	2,382	3,182	91.0	96.5	911	97.6
Biology	....	....	....	....	154	100.0
Bookkeeping	....	....	....	....	181	96.1
Business Organization	....	....	....	....	117	97.4
Chemistry	....	....	....	....	105	100.0
Civics	667	773	87.3	93.5	....	....
Commercial Arithmetic	16	213	87.5	98.1	....	....
Distributive Education	....	....	....	....	14	100.0
Economics	....	....	....	....	85	100.0
English	2,382	3,182	83.3	93.2	2,345	96.2
French	117	196	78.6	84.2	483	94.4
General Science	1,104	1,600	85.1	92.3	....	....
Geography	1,522	1,710	84.5	94.6	190	88.0
History	1,712	2,409	86.6	94.0	1,231	95.5
Home Economics	....	4,713	....	91.9	1,016	96.7
Hygiene	974	1,193	80.4	90.9	....	....
Industrial Arts	2,284	....	89.4	....	392	94.9
Junior Business Traning	349	770	93.1	86.1	....	....
Latin	88	142	98.9	99.3	202	94.6
Mathematics	2,363	2,941	80.7	87.8	129	97.7
Mechanical Drawing	1,179	....	89.1	....	189	97.9
Music	1,498	1,931	95.6	98.1	....	....
Office Practice	....	....	....	....	74	98.6
Physical Education	2,376	3,155	86.4	88.3	2,093	96.0
Physics	....	....	....	....	99	99.0
Plane Geometry	....	....	....	....	670	81.3
Reading	1,415	1,727	87.1	94.8	....	....
Solid Geometry	....	....	....	....	46	100.0
Spanish	273	313	86.8	89.8	352	99.7
Stenography	....	....	....	....	96	91.7
Trigonometry	....	....	....	....	152	94.7
Typing	16	213	93.8	94.4	520	97.5

TABLE 48
ACHIEVEMENTS BY SUBJECTS—COLORED JUNIOR AND
SENIOR HIGH SCHOOLS
SECOND SEMESTER, 1949-50

| Subject | JUNIOR HIGH | | | | SENIOR HIGH | |
| | Number Taking | | Per Cent Achieving | | | Per Cent |
	Boys	Girls	Boys	Girls	Number Taking	Achieving
Algebra	....	....	....	....	180	97.2
Art	2,607	3,335	93.7	96.7	1,120	96.7
Biology	....	....	....	....	895	88.8
Bookkeeping	....	....	....	....	255	93.7
Business Organization	....	....	....	....	181	92.8
Chemistry	....	....	....	....	472	98.7
Civics	467	567	90.4	94.9	....	....
Clerical Practice	....	....	....	....	92	100.0
Commercial Arithmetic	27	7	70.4	71.4	....	....
Distributive Education	....	....	....	....	45	100.0
Economics	....	....	....	....	72	98.6
English	2,608	3,435	87.9	94.4	2,517	94.2
French	140	218	83.6	88.5	564	89.7
General Science	1,375	1,850	90.4	93.9	....	....
Geography	1,491	1,858	88.3	92.5	288	91.0
History	2,141	2,862	89.1	94.7	1,283	95.8
Home Economics	....	4,864	....	92.7	1,081	93.3
Hygiene	1,021	1,297	83.2	92.6	....	....
Industrial Arts	2,347	....	89.0	....	369	91.3
Junior Business Training	498	891	92.4	95.8	....	....
Latin	74	153	95.9	91.5	218	97.2
Mathematics	2,489	3,350	83.9	91.4	123	97.6
Mechanical Drawing	1,282	....	91.3	....	263	94.7
Music	1,637	2,166	97.7	98.5	73	100.0
Office Machines	....	....	....	....	11	100.0
Office Practice	....	....	....	....	119	99.2
Physical Education	2,598	3,422	85.8	92.2	2,478	92.4
Physics	....	....	....	....	395	94.4
Plane Geometry	....	....	....	....	792	84.5
Reading	1,464	1,914	89.6	95.7	....	....
Solid Geometry	....	....	....	....	63	98.4
Spanish	220	219	91.8	93.6	627	93.3
Stenography	....	....	....	....	288	97.2
Trigonometry	....	....	....	....	142	99.3
Typing	39	240	89.7	97.5	488	94.1

TABLE 49
DEPARTMENT OF EDUCATION PERSONNEL, JUNE 30, 1949 AND 1950

Classification	1948-1949			1949-1950		
	Total	White	Colored	Total	White	Colored
TOTAL EMPLOYEES	**5,257**	**3,705**	**1,552**	**5,463**	**3,577**	**1,886**
Superintendent	1	1	....	1	1	....
Assistant Superintendent	6	5	1	6	5	1
Administrative Assistant	1	1	....	1	1	....
Director:						
Adult Education	1	1	....	1	1	....
Art	1	1	....	1	1	....
Education Supplies and						
Equipment	1	1	....	1	1	....
Music	1	1	....	1	1	....
Personnel	1	1	....	1	1	....
Phys. Education	1	1	....	1	1	....
Primary Grades and						
Kindergarten	1	1	....	1	1	....
Research	1	1	....	1	1	....
Special Education	1	1	....	1	1	....
Special Services	1	1	....	1	1	....
School Facilities	1	1	....	1	1	....
Assistant Director:						
Aptitude Testing	1	1	....	1	1	....
Curriculum	2	2	....	2	2	....
Guidance and Placement......	1	1	....	1	1	....
Research	2	2	....	2	2	....
Supervisors:						
Elementary	12	8	4	12	8	4
Junior High	1	1(a)	(a)	1	1(b)	(a)
Senior High	1	1(b)	....	1	1(a)	....
Supervisors—Departmental:						
Adult Education	1	....	1	1	....	1
Audio-Vis. Education	1	1	....	1	1	....
Business Division	1	1	....	....	....	....
Child Guidance	1	1	....	1	1	....
Commercial	1	1	....	1	1	....
Distributive Education	1	1	....	1	1	....
Educational Supplies and						
Equipment	4	4	...	4	4	....
Handwriting	1	1	....	1	1	....
Health and Phys. Education	1	1	....	1	1	....
Home Economics	1	1	....	1	1	....
Hygiene and Health						
Education	1	1	....	1	1	....

(a) Four supervisors on school payrolls.
(b) Three supervisors on school payrolls.

TABLE 49—(Continued)
DEPARTMENT OF EDUCATION PERSONNEL, JUNE 30, 1949 AND 1950

Classification	1948-1949			1949-1950		
	Total	White	Colored	Total	White	Colored
Supervisors (Continued)						
Industrial and Trade						
Education	3	3	....	3	3	....
Instrumental Music	1	1	....	1	1	....
Parent Education	1	1	....	1	1	....
School Libraries	1	1	....	1	1	....
Special Education	4	3	1	4	3	1
Shop Center and Occ.	1	1	....	1	1	....
Vocational Ed. (Adults)	1	1	....	1	1	....
Assistant Supervisors:						
Art	1	1	....	1	1	....
Educational Supplies and						
Equipment	1	1	....	1	1	....
English	....	(c)	....	....	(c)	....
Guidance	1	1	....	1	1	....
History	....	(c)	....	....	(c)	....
Mathematics	....	(c)	....	....	(c)	....
Music	1	1	....	1	1	....
Vocational Equip.	1	1	....	1	1	....
Specialists:						
Adult Education	....	....	....	1	1	....
Art	4	3	1(c)	4	3	1(c)
Music	5	4	1(c)	5	4	1(c)
Phys. Education	5	3	2	5	3	2
Personnel	1	1	....	1	1	....
Radio Education	1	1	....	1	1	....
Reading	4	2	2	4	2	2
Rehabilitation						
Counseling	1	1	....	1	1	....
Supplies and Equipment	4	4	....	6	6	....
Principals:						
Assigned to Business						
Office	1	1	....	1	1	....
Coppin Teachers College	1	....	1	1	....	1
Senior High	8	7	1	8	7	1
Vocational High	3	2	1	3	2	1
Gen. Vocational	4	3	1	6	4	2
Junior High	13	9	4	13	9	4
Occupational	1	1	....	....	....	....
Elementary	103	67	36	102	67	35

(c) One on school payroll.

TABLE 49—(Continued)

DEPARTMENT OF EDUCATION PERSONNEL, JUNE 30, 1949 AND 1950

Classification	1948-1949			1949-1950		
	Total	White	Colored	Total	White	Colored
Vice-Principals:						
Junior College	1	1	....	1	1	....
Senior High	14	12	2	15	13	2
Junior High	18	12	6	16	10	6
Occupational	1	1	....	1	1	....
Elementary	37	24	13	35	22	13
Teachers: (d)						
Assigned to Central Office	9	8	1	9	8	1
Coppin Teachers College....	7	....	7	7	....	7
Baltimore Junior College....	22	22	....	30	30	....
Senior High	595	503	92	604	507	97
Vocational High	104	67	37	102	67	35
General Vocational	60	44	16	73	43	30
Junior High	791	576	215	803	575	228
Occupational	84	52	32	88	55	33
Elementary(e)	1,907	1,186	721	2,038	1,260	778
Home and Hospital	14	9	5	14	10	4
Kindergarten	158	109	49	160	116	44
Lip Reading	4	3	1	3	2	1
Prekindergarten	9	6	3	12	6	6
Speech Correction	8	6	2	8	6	2
Visiting	21	16	5	21	15	6
Assistant - Business Division	1	1	....	1	1	....
Assistant Supv. Custodian	1	1	....	1	1	....
Aptitude Testing Assistant....	6	5	1	6	5	1
Audiometrist	1	1	....	1	1	....
Carpenter Foreman	2	2	....	2	2	....
Clerical and Custodial Staff (f)	1,031	765	266	1,045	534	511
Coordinator	1	1	....	3	2	1
Credit Examiner	1	1	....	1	1	....
District Supv. of School Buildings	9	9	....	11	11	....
Draftsman	4	4	....	4	4	....
General Supt. - Bldgs. and Grounds	1	1	....	1	1	....

(d) Includes substitutes, supervisors, and laboratory assistants.
(e) Exclusive of kindergarten and prekindergarten teachers.
(f) Includes part-time custodians.

TABLE 49—(Continued)
DEPARTMENT OF EDUCATION PERSONNEL, JUNE 30, 1949 AND 1950

Classification	1948-1949			1949-1950		
	Total	White	Colored	Total	White	Colored
Head Account Clerk..................	1	1	....	1	1	....
Home Visitor—Head	1	1	....	1	1	....
Home Visitor	21	16	5	22	17	5
Inspector of Bldgs....................	1	1	....	1	1	....
Junior Admn. Officer—						
Clerical	1	1	....	1	1	....
Junior Admn. Officer—						
Personnel	1	1	....	1	1	....
Junior Assoc. Engineer............	....	....	....	1	1	....
Piano Tuners	2	2	....	2	2	....
Physicians and Nurses............	45	35	10	46	35	11
Placement Counselors	7	5	2	7	5	2
Psychiatrists(g)	....	....	....	2	2	....
Psychologist	....	....	....	1	1	....
Psychometric Examiners	4	4	....	4	4	....
Research Assistant	3	3	....	3	3	....
Special Assistant	1	....	1	2	1	1
Senior Asst. Supt.—Warehouse	1	1	....	1	1	....
Senior Supervisor—						
Installations	1	1	....	1	1	....
Superintendent—Design and						
Construction	1	1	....	1	1	....
Superintendent—Repair						
Shop	1	1	....	1	1	....
Supervising Plant Engineers	2	2	....	2	2	....
Stock Handler	2	2	....	2	2	....
Storekeeper	2	2	....	3	3	....
Therapist	7	4	3	9	5	4
Typewriter Repairman	1	1	....	1	1	....

(g) Part time.
In addition to its regular employees, the Department of Education engages the services of hourly per diem carpenters, plumbers, and laborers, estimated at 234 for the year 1948-1949 and 205 for the year 1949-1950.

TABLE 50
Summary of Cases Referred to the Division of Aptitude Testing

Source and Reason for Referral	1948-1949 Number of Cases Total	White	Colored	1949-1950 Number of Cases Total	White	Colored
TOTAL	**15,356**	**10,075**	**5,281**	**16,117**	**10,546**	**5,571**
1. Referred by elementary schools						
a. For classification and recommendation for adjustment:						
3B	4	....	4	....	....	....
3A	4	....	4	....	....	....
4B	19	14	5	13	7	6
4A	39	26	13	54	38	16
5B	206	163	43	159	122	37
5A	389	253	136	283	218	65
6B	720	503	217	495	331	164
6A	886	458	338	695	474	221
Shop Center	335	93	242	314	104	210
Occupational	243	11	232	261	15	246
b. For shop center:						
1A	1	1	....	....	....	....
3B	8	1	7	....	....	....
3A	2	....	2	4	3	1
4B	14	7	7	6	2	4
4A	34	11	23	33	21	12
5B	85	45	40	74	42	32
5A	83	16	67	86	47	39
6B	89	11	78	50	21	29
6A	41	3	38	28	5	23
Opportunity	698	317	381	682	312	370
Special Center	5	....	5	5	5	....
Shop Center	104	58	46	89	44	45
Occupational	9	9	....	16	15	1
Other Sources	164	20	144	114	17	97
2. By Junior High Schools:						
7B	944	573	371	746	608	138
7A	846	733	113	659	506	153
8B	2,294	654	1,640	2,897	945	1,952
8A	1,136	1,036	100	677	608	69
9B	448	339	109	1,000	944	56
9A	489	411	78	326	279	47
Shop Center	14	....	14	....	....	....

TABLE 50—(Continued)
SUMMARY OF CASES REFERRED TO THE DIVISION OF APTITUDE TESTING

Source and Reason for Referral	1948-1949 Number of Cases			1949-1950 Number of Cases		
	Total	White	Colored	Total	White	Colored
3. By Senior High Schools:						
10B	77	54	23	293	282	11
10A	57	43	14	107	11	96
11B	12	1	11	33	21	12
11A	11	3	8	11	7	4
12B	8	2	6	3	2	1
12A	6	1	5	3	1	2
4. By Vocational Schools for entry or adjustment	85	85	....	29	20	9
5. By Division of Art Education and Schools for Art aptitude tests and scholarships	390	363	27	367	361	6
6. By Division of Music Education and Schools for Music aptitude tests and scholarships	561	501	60	1,123	763	360
7. By Division of Special Education for adjustment in Occupational classes	54	36	18	84	37	47
8. By Division of Special Services for Child Guidance Clinic	8	8	....	28	28	....
9. By Schools for Clerical aptitude tests	1,364	1,173	191	1,623	1,381	242
10. By Schools, non-residents	140	88	52	199	88	111
11. By Schools for College aptitude battery	....	....	....	580	....	580
12. By Private Schools	422	395	27	459	434	25
13. By Cheltenham and Md. Training Schools	58	21	37	80	48	32
14. Veterans and High School Seniors for adjustment in college or other schools	1,449	1,445	4	1,313	1,313	....
15. Candidates for Coppin Teachers College, for testing	286	....	286	....	....	....
16. From Other Sources for testing	15	....	15	16	16	....

TABLE 51
CASE LOAD OF THE DIVISION OF SPECIAL SERVICES

Item	1948-49	1949-50
Total number of active cases during the year....	3,376	3,601
Number closed during school year.........................	2,201	1,993
Number active as of next school year...................	1,175	1,608

TABLE 52
GRADE LEVEL, AGE, AND INTELLIGENCE OF PUPILS TREATED BY THE DIVISION OF SPECIAL SERVICES DURING 1948-49 AND 1949-50

Grade Level	No. of Cases	Age Level	No. of Cases	Intelligence	No. of Cases
Total 6,977		All 6,977		Total Cases...........6,977	
Grade 12.................	15	22........	1	Binet IQ	
Grade 11.................	32	19........	13	140-149...................	1
Grade 10.................	84	18........	19	130-139...................	25
Grade 9.................	229	17........	48	120-129...................	37
Grade 8.................	333	16........	210	110-119...................	120
Grade 7.................	595	15........1,229		100-109...................	261
Grade 6.................	358	14........1,190		90- 99...................	694
Grade 5.................	569	13........	901	80- 89...................	974
Grade 4.................	772	12........	702	70- 79,...............1,012	
Grade 3.................	738	11........	628	60- 69...................	507
Grade 2.................	534	10........	512	50- 59...................	133
Grade 1.................	360	9........	532	40- 49...................	26
Kindergarten	51	8........	486	30- 39...................	1
Vocational	187	7........	307		
Shop Center	728	6........	166		
Special Center......	23	5........	33		
Occupational	566				
Primary Opp.	344				
Inter. Opp.	439			Determined by	
Mixed Opp.	11			group or	
Sight Saving	4			performance	
Phys. Handicpd. ..	4			test 2,445	
Job Training	1			No record	741

TABLE 53
PRINCIPAL CHARACTERISTICS OF CASES TREATED IN THE
DIVISION OF SPECIAL SERVICES

Case Distribution	1948-1949			1949-1950		
	Total	White	Colored	Total	White	Colored
Total Cases	**3,376**	**2,270**	**1,106**	**3,601**	**2,560**	**1,041**
Symptomatic Analysis						
Aggressive behavior....	822	620	202	934	747	187
Poor attendance	1,780	1,111	669	1,688	1,149	539
Stealing	....	....	....	3	3	....
Sex offenses	4	2	2	10	6	4
Withdrawing behavior	48	35	13	53	38	15
Educational						
maladjustment	285	193	92	516	326	190
Home problems	238	167	71	211	153	58
Economic behavior	1	1	....	4	4	....
Other reasons	198	141	57	182	134	48
Referrals to Other Agencies						
Psychiatric clinic	154	103	51	133	109	24
Medical clinic	147	61	86	134	60	74
Social agencies	94	64	30	56	42	14
Juvenile court	273	197	76	292	193	99
Public welfare agency	168	83	85	164	93	71
Recreational agency ..	38	18	20	43	21	22
Child Study center......	16	16	....	17	17	....
Action on Cases...............	**456**	**333**	**123**	**424**	**322**	**102**
To other schools...........	262	196	66	210	164.	46
To other curricula......	91	46	45	131	80	51
To Highwood	48	48	....	71	71	....
Reading clinic	11	7	4	12	7	5
Work permit	44	36	8	....	....	....
Interviews						
Periodic	1,056	613	443	....	....	....
Authoritative	943	564	379	736	478	258
By visiting teacher......	1,471	997	474	2,544	1,831	713
By psychologists	292	266	26	454	397	57
By staff psychiatrists	24	22	2	154	121	33
Estimate of Adjustment						
Improved	57.0%	55.7%	59.6%	57.3%	53.1%	67.5%
Unchanged	39.3%	39.7%	38.5%	35.8%	40.6%	23.9%
Deteriorating	3.7%	4.6%	1.9%	3.9%	4.5%	2.5%
No contact	....	....	....	3.0%	1.8%	6.1%

TABLE 54

COMPARATIVE STATISTICS ON PLACEMENT SERVICE FOR THE YEARS
ENDING JUNE 30, 1949 AND JUNE 30, 1950 RESPECTIVELY—
WHITE SCHOOLS

Month	Registrants 1949	1950	Jobs to be Filled 1949	1950	Referrals 1949	1950	Placements 1949	1950
GRAND TOTAL	1,793	1,674	1,927	1,739	5,395	6,105	969	1,015
TOTAL BOYS	777	777	759	761	2,133	2,535	396	411
July	12	7	55	41	132	121	67	53
August	7	10	63	48	155	191	35	32
September	8	25	73	80	90	79	17	35
October	73	121	37	37	58	70	24	16
November	96	86	39	31	40	78	13	18
December	95	32	26	25	33	41	11	14
January	33	56	154	81	453	385	14	17
February	50	19	55	61	277	301	95	70
March	140	135	-40	57	136	176	23	40
April	173	133	26	52	75	112	22	16
May	51	140	108	133	255	474	19	10
June	39	13	83	115	429	507	56	90
TOTAL GIRLS	1,016	897	1,168	978	3,262	3,570	573	604
July	8	6	99	51	311	183	58	53
August	1	2	108	62	160	260	38	31
September	11	14	35	70	141	233	26	45
October	137	115	64	35	76	122	15	25
November	177	107	54	30	43	79	19	9
December	44	107	22	29	32	40	8	10
January	41	19	260	138	787	638	8	14
February	22	14	99	99	497	428	160	133
March	180	67	67	46	142	193	38	34
April	190	218	43	77	61	55	12	13
May	184	219	150	193	416	694	10	4
June	21	9	167	148	596	645	181	233
Part Time and Temporary								
Boys	255	132	208	99	409	255	98	52
Girls	279	302	209	188	338	288	169	181
Work-Study Program								
Boys	9	14	9	9	14	14	6	7
Girls	168	112	169	94	336	213	159	98

TABLE 55
COMPARATIVE STATISTICS ON PLACEMENT SERVICE FOR THE YEARS
ENDING JUNE 30, 1949 AND JUNE 30, 1950 RESPECTIVELY—
COLORED SCHOOLS

Month	Registrants 1949	1950	Jobs to be Filled 1949	1950	Referrals 1949	1950	Placements 1949	1950
GRAND TOTAL	600	677	177	168	416	361	113	109
TOTAL BOYS....	195	258	60	91	101	197	34	54
July	2	1	3	3	5	8	4	3
August	0	0	9	1	7	1	2	1
September	2	7	6	8	11	13	5	6
October	1	19	7	4	6	9	2	2
November	39	70	1	0	1	2	3	1
December	36	4	1	1	2	1	0	1
January	16	34	6	4	17	13	1	2
February	3	5	4	5	12	13	3	4
March	1	8	8	22	14	22	6	6
April	1	43	5	12	5	29	4	10
May	87	62	3	13	7	32	1	7
June	7	5	7	18	14	54	3	11
TOTAL GIRLS..	405	419	117	77	315	164	79	55
July	5	3	6	2	8	3	2	2
August	2	0	10	2	16	2	7	2
September	7	11	10	15	21	38	7	13
October	2	39	9	5	19	9	8	2
November	133	92	3	4	7	10	2	5
December	33	40	3	2	29	2	3	1
January	14	29	7	7	84	19	2	1
February	7	6	7	5	12	11	2	8
March	6	8	26	9	41	9	22	6
April	5	86	15	3	26	11	12	1
May	147	99	14	12	36	30	5	12
June	44	6	7	11	16	20	7	2
Part Time and Temporary Boys	447	440	127	108	172	167	101	101
Girls	599	578	106	120	171	173	100	112
Work-Study Program Boys	0	0	0	0	0	0	0	0
Girls	0	0	0	0	0	0	0	0

TABLE 56

CLASSIFICATIONS OF JOBS BY OCCUPATIONAL GROUPS, AGE, AND
EDUCATIONAL REQUIREMENTS AS INDICATED BY EMPLOYERS'
ORDERS RECEIVED BY THE PUBLIC SCHOOL PLACEMENT
SERVICE, PLACEMENTS MADE BETWEEN
JULY 1, 1948, AND JUNE 30, 1950—ALL SCHOOLS

	1948-1949		1949-1950	
	Male	Female	Male	Female
ALL CLASSIFICATIONS COMBINED—				
Orders Received	838	1,306	852	1,055
Placements	541	752	465	659
Age Requirements:				
16-17	516	1,184	458	941
18 and Over	307	119	394	114
Under 16	15	3	0	0
Educational Requirements:				
Junior College Graduation	14	0	16	1
High School Graduation	599	1,258	617	989
Occupational or Vocational	65	17	58	23
Not Specified	160	31	161	42
ALL CLASSIFICATIONS COMBINED— WHITE				
Orders Received	759	1,168	761	978
Placements	396	573	411	604
Age Requirements:				
16-17	450	1,073	411	895
18 and Over	296	95	350	83
Under 16	13	0	0	0
Educational Requirements:				
Junior College Graduation	14	0	16	1
High School Graduation	554	1,142	565	933
Occupational or Vocational	61	13	46	14
Not Specified	130	13	134	30
ALL CLASSIFICATIONS COMBINED— COLORED				
Orders Received	79	138	91	77
Placements	145	179	54	55
Age Requirements:				
16-17	66	111	47	46
18 and Over	11	24	44	31
Under 16	2	3	0	0
Educational Requirements:				
High School Graduation	45	116	52	56
Occupational or Vocational	4	4	12	9
Not Specified	30	18	27	12

TABLE 57

CLASSIFICATIONS OF JOBS BY OCCUPATIONAL GROUPS, AGE, AND
EDUCATIONAL REQUIREMENTS AS INDICATED BY EMPLOYERS'
ORDERS RECEIVED BY THE PUBLIC SCHOOL PLACEMENT
SERVICE, PLACEMENTS MADE BETWEEN
JULY 1, 1948, AND JUNE 30, 1950—WHITE SCHOOLS

	1948-1949 Male	1948-1949 Female	1949-1950 Male	1949-1950 Female
CLERICAL: All types of junior office workers; e.g., stenographers, typists, office machine operators, and clerks, such as office boys, runners, and file clerks.				
Orders Received	293	1,127	329	922
Placements	130	564	143	579
Age Requirements:				
16-17	201	1,038	218	847
18 and Over	85	89	111	75
Under 16	7	0	0	0
Educational Requirements:				
Junior College Graduation	6	0	8	0
High School Graduation	231	1,114	287	915
Occupational or Vocational	5	2	2	1
Not Specified	51	11	32	6
HOUSEHOLD AND DOMESTIC SERVICE: All types of workers in private homes; e.g., mothers' helpers, child care workers, cooks, light housekeeping helpers, and maids.				
Orders Received	0	1	0	1
Placements	0	0	0	0
Age Requirements:				
16-17	0	1	0	1
18 and Over	0	0	0	0
Educational Requirements:				
High School Graduation	0	1	0	0
Not Specified	0	0	0	1
PERSONAL SERVICE: All types of service workers outside of the home; e. g., waitresses, hotel and restaurant workers, beauticians, and bootblacks.				
Orders Received	0	3	0	2
Placements	0	1	0	0
Age Requirements:				
16-17	0	3	0	2
Educational Requirements:				
Junior College Graduation	0	0	0	0
High School Graduation	0	0	0	0
Occupational or Vocational	0	2	0	1
Not Specified	0	1	0	1

TABLE 57—Continued
CLASSIFICATIONS OF JOBS AND PLACEMENTS MADE BETWEEN JULY 1, 1948, AND JUNE 30, 1950—WHITE SCHOOLS

	1948-1949		1949-1950	
	Male	Female	Male	Female
SALES AND STOCK: Junior salesmen, store clerks, and stockworkers of all kinds, including receiving, order filling, wrapping, packing, and shipping clerks.				
Orders Received	130	8	151	9
Placements	81	0	92	5
Age Requirements:				
16-17	94	7	93	7
18 and Over	35	1	58	2
Under 16	1	0	0	0
Educational Requirements:				
Junior College Graduation	1	0	6	1
High School Graduation	84	7	97	5
Occupational or Vocational	4	0	4	0
Not Specified	41	1	44	3
SEMI-PROFESSIONAL AND TECHNICAL: Junior workers, whose positions are somewhat professional or technical in character (tutors, camp counselors, playground workers, junior and apprentice draftsmen, surveyors' and laboratory assistants, and student technicians).				
Orders Received	153	16	106	12
Placements	79	5	53	6
Age Requirements:				
16-17	61	13	39	11
18 and Over	87	3	67	1
Under 16	5	0	0	0
Educational Requirements:				
Junior College Graduation	3	0	2	0
High School Graduation	141	16	103	12
Not Specified	9	0	1	0
TRADES AND INDUSTRIAL: Apprentices and helpers in various skilled trades; also semi-skilled and unskilled workers in factories, plants, and shops.				
Orders Received	183	13	175	32
Placements	106	3	123	14
Age Requirements:				
16-17	94	11	61	27
18 and Over	89	2	114	5
Under 16	0	0	0	0
Educational Requirements:				
Junior College Graduation	4	0	0	0
High School Graduation	98	4	78	0
Occupational or Vocational	52	9	40	13
Not Specified	29	0	57	19

TABLE 58
Classifications of Jobs by Occupational Groups, Age, and Educational Requirements as Indicated by Employers' Orders Received by the Public School Placement Service, Placements Made Between July 1, 1948, and June 30, 1950—Colored Schools

	1948-1949 Male	1948-1949 Female	1949-1950 Male	1949-1950 Female
CLERICAL: All types of junior office workers; e.g., stenographers, typists, office machine operators, and clerks, such as office boys, runners, and file clerks.				
Orders Received	17	48	7	16
Placements	14	46	2	7
Age Requirements:				
16-17	8	15	3	5
18 and Over	9	33	4	11
Under 16	0	0	0	0
Educational Requirements:				
High School Graduation	14	48	7	16
Occupational or Vocational	0	0	0	0
Not Specified	3	0	0	0
HOUSEHOLD AND DOMESTIC SERVICE: All types of workers in private homes; e.g., mothers' helpers, child care workers, cooks, light housekeeping helpers, and maids.				
Orders Received	0	5	0	7
Placements	0	23	0	4
Age Requirements:				
16-17	0	1	0	4
18 and Over	0	4	0	3
Educational Requirements:				
High School Graduation	0	1	0	0
Occupational or Vocational	0	0	0	1
Not Specified	0	4	0	6
PERSONAL SERVICE: All types of service workers outside of the home; e.g., waitresses, hotel and restaurant workers, beauticians, and bootblacks.				
Orders Received	33	28	34	22
Placements	106	47	25	17
Age Requirements:				
16-17	31	27	22	12
18 and Over	0	0	12	10
Under 16	2	1	0	0
Educational Requirements:				
High School Graduation	12	16	15	17
Occupational or Vocational	2	2	3	0
Not Specified	19	10	16	5

TABLE 58—Continued
CLASSIFICATIONS OF JOBS AND PLACEMENTS MADE BETWEEN JULY 1, 1948, AND JUNE 30, 1950—COLORED SCHOOLS

	1948-1949		1949-1950	
	Male	Female	Male	Female
SALES AND STOCK: Junior salesmen, store clerks, and stock workers of all kinds, including receiving, order filling, wrapping, packing, and shipping clerks.				
Orders Received	19	13	32	13
Placements	14	14	19	9
Age Requirements:				
16-17	19	6	12	9
18 and Over	0	7	20	4
Under 16	0	0	0	0
Educational Requirements:				
High School Graduation..............................	17	13	24	12
Occupational or Vocational.........................	0	0	0	1
Not Specified	2	0	8	0
SEMI-PROFESSIONAL AND TECHNICAL: Junior workers whose positions are somewhat professional or technical in character (tutors, camp counselors, playground workers, junior and apprentice draftsmen, surveyors' and laboratory assistants, and student technicians).				
Orders Received	2	37	5	9
Placements	1	44	3	9
Age Requirements:				
16-17	2	24	2	7
18 and Over	0	13	3	2
Under 16	0	0	0	0
Educational Requirements:				
High School Graduation..............................	2	37	5	7
Not Specified ....:.......................................	0	0	0	2
TRADES AND INDUSTRIAL: Apprentices and helpers in various skilled trades; also semi-skilled and unskilled workers in factories, plants, and shops.				
Orders Received	8	6	13	10
Placements	10	5	5	9
Age Requirements:				
16-17	2	0	8	9
18 and Over	6	6	5	1
Under 16	0	0	0	0
Educational Requirements:				
High School Graduation..............................	0	1	1	4
Occupational or Vocational.........................	2	2	9	5
Not Specified	6	3	3	1

TABLE 59
GENERAL SUMMARY OF SUMMER SCHOOLS [1]

Item	Session of 1948			Session of 1949		
	Total	White	Colored	Total	White	Colored
ENROLLMENT—TOTAL	**3,686**	**2,801**	**885**	**4,222**	**3,182**	**1,040**
Review Schools	3,134	2,503	631	3,600	2,808	792
Senior High	2,139	1,886	253	2,359	2,059	300
Junior High	995	617	378	1,241	749	492
Advanced Schools	552	298	254	622	374	248
Senior High	172	92	80	136	97	39
Junior High	....	....	....	81	79	2
Demonstration	380	206	174	405	198	207
NET ROLL—TOTAL	**3,421**	**2,566**	**855**	**3,865**	**2,886**	**979**
Review Schools	2,895	2,288	607	3,275	2,536	739
Senior High	1,997	1,745	252	2,166	1,877	289
Junior High	898	543	355	1,109	659	450
Advanced Schools	526	278	248	590	350	240
Senior High	163	84	79	129	91	38
Junior High	....	....	....	.65	63	2
Demonstration	363	194	169	396	196	200
AVERAGE NET ROLL —TOTAL	**3,540**	**2,668**	**872**	**3,958**	**2,990**	**968**
Senior High	2,234	1,905	329	2,352	2,050	302
Junior High	938	568	370	1,205	744	461
Demonstration	367	195	172	401	197	204
AVERAGE ATTENDANCE [2] —TOTAL	**3,388**	**2,561**	**827**	**3,743**	**2,844**	**899**
Senior High	2,144	1,831	313	2,231	1,951	280
Junior High	885	539	346	1,127	701	426
Demonstration	359	191	168	385	192	193
TEACHERS—TOTAL	**81**	**59**	**22**	**87**	**64**	**23**
Senior High	44	37	7	44	39	5
Junior High	21	13	8	27	16	11
Demonstration	16	9	7	16	9	7
PRINCIPALS[3]—TOTAL	**5**	**3**	**2**	**5**	**3**	**2**
Senior High	2	1	1	2	1	1
Junior High	1	1	....	1	1	....
Demonstration	2	1	1	2	1	1

[1] Summer sessions of the Baltimore Junior College enrolled 55 in 1948 and 92 in 1949.
[2] Number of days in session: 1948, 30; 1949, 29.
[3] Also number and distribution of schools.

TABLE 60

CENSUS OF CHILDREN BETWEEN THE AGES OF 5 AND 18 YEARS AS
REPORTED BY THE BALTIMORE POLICE DEPARTMENT

Age	NOVEMBER, 1948			NOVEMBER, 1949		
	Total	Physically Normal	Physically Handicapped	Total	Physically Normal	Physically Handicapped
TOTAL	138,438	137,771	667	141,434	140,769	665
5..............	12,005	11,978	27	10,965	10,936	29
6..............	13,249	13,203	46	13,957	13,914	43
7..............	11,906	11,858	48	13,466	13,409	57
8..............	11,142	11,082	60	12,431	12,368	63
9..............	10,561	10,507	54	11,017	10,954	63
10..............	10,628	10,581	47	10,712	10,669	43
11..............	10,004	9,955	49	10,589	10,532	57
12..............	9,958	9,899	59	10,535	10,471	64
13..............	10,076	10,014	62	9,876	9,823	53
14..............	9,875	9,810	65	9,922	9,874	48
15..............	9,174	9,113	61	9,368	9,302	66
16..............	8,668	8,624	44	8,284	8,243	41
17..............	7,078	7,047	31	7,148	7,121	27
18..............	4,114	4,100	14	3,164	3,153	11

TABLE 61

FOLLOW-UP OF FORMER STUDENTS WHO GRADUATED IN FEBRUARY AND
JUNE OF 1948 AND 1949, RESPECTIVELY

Activity	1948			1949		
	Total	White	Colored	Total	White	Colored
TOTAL GRADUATES	3,087	2,596	491	3,541	2,843	698
Advanced Study:						
Full-time[1]	1,006	837	169	1,145	956	189
Part-time[2]	(191)	(188)	(3)	(225)	(219)	(6)
Employed	949	846	103	1,260	1,135	125
Military Service	11	4	7	61	49	12
Unemployed	9	2	7	168	73	95
At home and other...........	67	33	34	36	28	8
No report	1,045	874	171	871	602	269

[1] The number of graduates in schools of higher education is determined by direct reports from the schools attended. The number in other occupations is based on postal card returns.

[2] Courses taken by graduates who otherwise are employed or at home and are so counted.

TABLE 62

Cost of Operating Schools for the Two Years Ending June 30, 1949 and 1950, Respectively—Expenditures by the Department of Education Only

Character of Service	1948-1949	1949-1950
TOTAL EXPENDITURES	$21,233,992.07	$24,117,483.34
Capital outlay	45,652.47	221,286.99
Current expense	21,188,339.60	23,896,196.35
General control	776,972.17	812,763.68
Instruction:		
Day Schools[1]	16,500,463.79	18,270,999.05
Summer schools	29,673.36	24,766.96
Adult education	976,303.53	1,001,779.35
Auxiliary services [2]	207,597.78	305,169.74
Operation of plant	2,033,227.37	2,316,666.28
Maintenance of plant[3]	654,714.68	1,149,966.08
Fixed charges	9,386.92	14,085.21

[1] Includes also inventory, home and hospital teaching. Continuation classes, merged with Distributive Education, are transferred to Adult Education.
[2] Promotion of health, transportation, etc.
[3] Includes inventory.

TABLE 63

Expenditures by Other City Departments for Public Education

Disbursing Agent and Object	1948-1949	1949-1950
TOTAL	$5,452,343.75	$7,713,523.52
Health Department		
Medical-dental inspection, nurse service	88,054.00	119,227.00
City Register		
Interest on loans	493,300.00	460,765.00
Payments into school sinking fund	5,400.00	5,400.00
Bond retirement	1,079,000.00	1,129,000.00
City Comptroller		
Insurance on buildings and equipment	23,138.12	25,000.00
Gross contributions account pensions	1,551,967.00	1,883,589.00
Expenditures from 4th, 5th, and 6th School Loans:		
School sites	494,723.05	568,039.75
Buildings	361,902.05	2,279,028.98
Engineering and Population Studies	21,014.29	18,743.50
Kirk Avenue Athletic Field	228,090.22	31,226.33
Expenditures from Equipment Loan	1,105,755.02	1,193,503.96

Items	All Day Schools	Elementary	Junior High
General Control:[2]			
Salaries ....$	556,078.35	$ 300,079.66	$ 114,928.72
Other Expenses	220,893.82	119,202.17	45,653.72
Total ....$	776,972.17	$ 419,281.83	$ 160,582.44
Instruction Service:			
Salaries—			
Supervisors ....$	361,109.05	$ 219,910.87	$ 70,438.74
Salaries—Principals			
and teachers	15,365,971.41	8,234,654.29	3,291,394.58
Textbooks	112,404.42	54,775.30	31,656.78
School library			
books	10,398.12	3,580.95	3,443.19
·ducational			
supplies	188,214.40	78,062.20	43,076.91
Other expenses	315,299.41	164,598.47	70,237.75
Total $16,353,396.81		$ 8,755,582.08	$ 3,510,247.95
Auxiliary Services:			
Promotion of			
health ....$	92,187.42	$ 14,431.81	$ 32,302.16
Physical education	27,251.38	....	....
Public lunches	47,404.31	47,404.31	....
Transportation	35,497.11	31,931.42	754.26
Community services ..	5,257.56	5,257.56	....
Total ....$	207,597.78	$ 99,025.10	$ 33,056.42
Operation of School Plant:			
Wages of janitors,			
etc. ....$	1,344,320.48	$ 751,445.01	$ 249,628.85
Fuel, lighting,			
supplies, etc.	688,906.89	381,448.22	87,795.15
Total ....$	2,033,227.37	$ 1,132,893.23	$ 337,424.00
Maintenance of School Plant:			
Buildings and grounds—			
Salaries ....$	69,252.93	$ 55,582.39	$ 7,236.93
Supplies	381,134.69	227,172.97	54,953.38
Janitors' equipment....	3,003.19	1,909.56	. 651.99
Educational			
equipment	88,484.83	42,510.80	16,332.43
Other expenses	31,718.54	24,634.02	3,588.18
Total ....$	573,594.18	$ 351,809.74	$ 32,762.91
Fixed Charges:			
Rent ....$	9,386.92	$ 9,386.92	....
Grand Total $19,954,175.23		$10,767,978.90	$ 4,124,073.72

[1] This table continued on page 161. Does not include inventory charges.
[2] Prorated proportionately to the distribution of direct charges to the several types of schools.

TABLE 64—Continued

CURRENT OPERATING EXPENSES OF FULL-TIME DAY SCHOOLS, 1948-49
DEPARTMENT OF EDUCATION ONLY .

	Senior High	Vocational	Occupational	Teachers College
General Control:[3]				
Salaries	$ 101,728.46	$ 26,001.41	$ 11,839.80	$ 1,500.30
Other expenses	40,410.12	10,328.66	4,703.18	595.97
Total	$ 142,138.58	$ 36,330.07	$ 16,542.98	$ 2,096.27
Instruction Service:				
Salaries—				
Supervisors	$ 31,141.32	$ 23,038.77	$ 7,345.35	$ 9,234.00
Principals and teachers.	2,810,887.83	624,676.95	366,253.09	38,104.67
Textbooks	20,989.54	3,247.41	1,354.98	380.41
School library books	2,168.97	1,088.26	13.95	102.80
Educational supplies	27,433.45	26,871.03	12,462.38	308.43
Other expenses	54,183.14	21,726.54	1,823.67	2,729.84
Total	$2,946,804.25	$700,648.96	$389,253.42	$50,860.15
Auxiliary Services:				
Promotion of health	$ 34,223.00	$ 10,939.95	$ 5.06	$ 285.44
Physical education	24,494.72	2,533.11	....	223.55
Public lunches	....	....	....	....
Transportation	1,531.92	378.83	900.68	....
Community services	....	....	....	....
Total	$ 60,249.64	$ 13,851.89	$ 905.74	$ 508.99
Operation of School Plant:				
Wages of janitors, etc.	$ 248,068.76	$ 84,383.58	$ 10,794.28	$ ....
Fuel, lighting, supplies, etc.	163,234.90	52,921.73	3,195.05	311.84
Total	$ 411,303.66	$137,305.31	$ 13,989.33	$ 311.84
Maintenance of School Plant:				
Buildings and grounds—				
Salaries	$ 4,688.43	$ 983.40	$ 761.78	$ ....
Supplies	61,696.44	35,232.73	2,063.42	15.75
Janitors' equipment	338.93	78.81	23.90	....
Educational equipment	20,540.94	8,192.36	863.29	45.01
Other expenses	2,638.89	404.64	452.81	....
Total	$ 89,903.63	$ 44,891.94	$ 4,165.20	$ 60.76
Fixed Charges:				
Rent	....	....	....	....
Grand Total	$3,650,399.76	$933,028.17	$424,856.67	$53,838.01

[3] Prorated proportionately to the distribution of direct charges to the several types of schools.

TABLE 65

CURRENT OPERATING EXPENSES OF FULL-TIME DAY SCHOOLS, 1949-50
. DEPARTMENT OF EDUCATION ONLY [1]

Items	All Day Schools	Elementary	Junior High
General Control:[2]			
Salaries	$ 598,269.96	$ 333,000.40	$ 119,774.85
Other expenses	214,493.72	119,388.39	42,942.06
Total	$ 812,763.68	$ 452,388.79	$ 162,716.91
Instruction Service:			
Salaries—			
Supervisors	$ 430,893.65	$ 259,175.32	$ 103,299.62
Salaries—Principals and teachers	16,840,825.28	9,156,992.01	3,515,124.22
Textbooks	96,613.02	69,498.49	10,574.15
School library books	37,318.87	23,018.77	6,856.18
Educational supplies..	383,302.67	230,134.27	65,032.06
Other expenses	344,774.00	174,016.48	84,179.23
Total	$18,133,727.49	$ 9,912,835.34	$3,785,065.46
Auxiliary Services:			
Promotion of health	$ 94,817.53	$ 12,158.08	$ 48,399.37
Physical education	86,874.87	....	....
Public lunches	59,537.37	56,684.82	....
Transportation	58,841.01	56,267.83	71.55
Community services ..	5,098.96	5,098.96	....
Total	$ 305,169.74	$ 130,209.69	$ 48,470.92
Operation of School Plant:			
Wages of janitors, etc.	$ 1,607,662.50	$ 989,116.23	$ 281,373.39
Fuel, lighting, supplies, etc.	709,033.78	387,874.52	121,768.96
Total	$ 2,316,666.28	$ 1,376,990.75	$ 403,142.35
Maintenance of School Plant:			
Buildings and Grounds—			
Salaries	$ 71,143.78	$ 56,950.60	$ 7,320.70
Supplies	783,811.64	514,278.36	103,507.70
Janitors' equipment ..	11,309.18	7,036.21	1,619.17
Educational equipment	70,406.87	35,055.52	11,090.96
Other expenses	148,930.18	119,226.88	15,258.01
Total	$ 1,085,773.53	$ 732,547.57	$ 138,796.54
Fixed Charges:			
Rent and insurance	$ 14,085.21	$ 12,306.17	....
Grand Total	$22,668,185.93	$12,617,278.31	$4,538,192.18

[1] This table continued on page 163. Does not include inventory charges.
[2] Prorated proportionately to the distribution of direct charges to the several types of schools

TABLE 65—Continued

CURRENT OPERATING EXPENSES OF FULL-TIME DAY SCHOOLS, 1949-50
DEPARTMENT OF EDUCATION ONLY

Items	Senior High	Vocational	Occupational	Teachers College
General Control:[3]				
Salaries	$ 100,071.82	$ 30,677.80	$ 13,014.30	$ 1,730.79
Other expenses ..	35,878.08	10,998.70	4,665.93	620.56
Total	$ 135,949.90	$ 41,676.50	$ 17,680.23	$ 2,351.35
Instruction Service:				
Salaries—				
Supervisors	$ 46,613.88	$ 10,493.45	$ 7,929.46	$ 3,381.92
Principals and teachers	2,912,573.93	802,173.50	408,187.25	45,774.37
Textbooks	7,994.50	7,125.53	1,420.35	....
School library books	5,763.49	1,262.63	288.00	129.80
Educational supplies	42,837.87	34,058.85	10,424.40	815.22
Other expenses ..	57,027.95	22,237.89	3,750.55	3,561.90
Total	$3,072,811.62	$ 877,351.85	$432,000.01	$53,663.21
Auxiliary Services:				
Promotion of health	$ 22,456.45	$ 11,692.65	$ 3.18	$ 107.80
Physical education	76,310.60	9,878.92	....	685.35
Public lunches ...	....	....	2,852.55	....
Transportation ..	1,192.63	257.00	1,052.00	....
Community services	....	....	....	....
Total .... $	99,959.68	$ 21,828.57	$ 3,907.73	$ 793.15
Operation of School Plant:				
Wages of janitors, etc.	$ 228,697.14	$ 92,292.04	$ 12,182.44	$ 4,001.26
Fuel, lighting, supplies, etc. ..	127,692.51	63,741.31	6,517.42	1,409.06
Total	$ 356,389.65	$ 156,033.35	$ 18,699.86	$ 5,410.32
Maintenance of School Plant:				
Buildings and Grounds—				
Salaries	$ 4,610.12	$ 1,159.64	$ 1,102.72	....
Supplies	95,722.30	50,938.19	16,311.11	3,053.98
Janitors' equipment	1,013.96	1,639.84	....	....
Educational equipment	14,618.78	8,560.66	947.66	133.29
Other expenses ..	9,633.44	2,506.16	2,305.69	....
Total	$ 125,598.60	$ 64,804.49	$ 20,667.18	$ 3,359.15
Fixed Charges:				
Rent and insurance .... $	944.11	$ 676.80	$ 158.13	....
Grand Total	$3,791,653.56	$1,162,371.56	$493,113.14	$65,577.18

[3] Prorated proportionately to the distribution of direct charges to the several types of schools.

TABLE 66
ADULT EDUCATION AND SUMMER SCHOOLS, 1948 AND 1949

| Type of School | 1948-1949 | | 1949-1950 | |
	Adult Education	Summer Schools 1948	Adult Education	Summer Schools 1949
TOTAL	$976,303.53	$29,673.36	$1,001,779.35	$24,766.96
Senior High	144,647.91	14,042.38	157,189.66	14,447.69
Junior High	17,722.35	6,330.57	25,110.91	7,217.04
Elementary	32,083.78	9,300.41	32,522.82	3,102.23
Americanization ..	17,065.29		25,186.54	
Parent Education..	26,694.45		22,907.56	
Vocational	46,002.75		48,914.08	
Trade Extension ..	56,114.24		57,486.37	
Veterans Training	500,651.91		491,274.27	
Junior College	135,320.85		141,187.14	

TABLE 67
SOURCES OF INCOME OTHER THAN MUNICIPAL TAXATION, TOGETHER WITH AMOUNTS RECEIVED BY CITY COMPTROLLER ON ACCOUNT OF PUBLIC SCHOOLS DURING THE YEARS ENDING JUNE 30, 1949 AND JUNE 30, 1950

Source	June 30, 1949	June 30, 1950
GRAND TOTAL	$5,455,664.39	$5,805,652.93
Total—From State of Maryland..........	5,379,134.80	5,689,525.31
Part Payment of Salaries	232,478.65	277,597.65
Federal Vocational Fund	82,868.15	66,047.47
Physically Handicapped Children	10,000.00	6,255.70
Teachers' Pensions	1,226,535.00	1,367.809.00
Vocational Rehabilitation	4,383.33	4,500.00
Basic Aid per Classroom Unit	1,471,353.03	1,591,046.97
Basic Aid per Pupil	2,097,200.00	2,135,393.63
Incentive Fund for Buildings	244,316.64	196,253.00
Junior College	10,000.00	44,621.89
Total—Miscellaneous Revenues	76,529.59	116,127.62
Tuition—Non-resident Pupils	50,189.03	63,968.14
School Board Revenue	1,037.74	4,064.25
Intestate Estates Fund	25,302.82	48,095.23

TABLE 68

VALUATION OF SCHOOL PROPERTIES AS OF JUNE 30, 1950 [1]

Description	Land	Structures	Total
TOTAL	$9,736,614.95	$49,256,082.80	$58,992,697.75
Administration			
Buildings ....White	44,232.00	326,805.73	371,037.73
Colored	....	23,315.00	23,315.00
Elementary Schools White	3,292,470.52	18,149,875.46	21,442,345.98
Colored	789,307.87	2,814,943.70	3,604,251.57
Junior High Schools White	951,699.16	7,579,097.39	8,530,796.55
Colored	288,804.76	1,097,458.33	1,386,263.09
Senior High Schools White	840,233.60	9,474,212.97	10,314,446.57
Colored	277,147.60	1,865,936.65	2,143,084.25
Vocational Schools...White	383,321.00	603,663.00	986,984.00
Colored	17,553.00	297,709.00	315,262.00
Pre-Vocational Schools			
White	14,054.00	90,441.00	104,495.00
Colored	....	....	....
Schools for Handicapped			
Children ....White	89,241.86	611,513.34	700,755.20
Colored	79,044.68	298,549.16	377,593.84
Portable Schools ....White	2,087.16	274,946.61	277,033.77
Colored	....	81,494.00	81,494.00
Work in Progress [2] White	1,194,985.05	1,590,616.40	2,785,601.45
Colored	1,218,862.16	1,136,101.89	2,354,964.05
Equipment	....	2,339,416.20	2,339,416.20
Engineering Survey	....	16,514.00	16,514.00
Warehouse—			
Main Building	43,256.53	225,875.97	269,132.50
Portable Annex	....	7,421.00	7,421.00
Repair Shop—			
(Included in 503)	....	33,806.00	33,806.00
Storage Building	48,523.00	105,255.00	153,778.00
Abandoned Schools	161,791.00	211,115.00	372,906.00

[1] Data supplied by Bureau of Control and Accounts. Valuation figures here shown are not comparable with those reported prior to 1934.
[2] In this account are carried amounts expended for land and structures for which final valuation has not been determined.

TABLE 69

COST PER PUPIL IN AVERAGE DAILY ATTENDANCE FOR THE SCHOOL YEAR
1948-49 IN TWENTY-TWO CITIES OVER 300,000 POPULATION [1]

City	Total Yearly Current Expense	Rank
New York	$291.24	1
Rochester	280.30	2
San Francisco	279.19	3
Boston	257.87	4
Los Angeles	252.25	5
Chicago	247.25	6
Washington	246.89	7
Cincinnati	239.79	8
Minneapolis	238.77	9
Portland	231.45	10
Detroit	229.97	11
Baltimore	227.56	12
Pittsburgh	226.45	13
Denver	225.52	14
Cleveland	224.61	15
St. Louis	224.47	16
Kansas City	218.35	17
Philadelphia	213.41	18
Seattle	205.87	19
New Orleans	172.87	20
Houston	158.41	21
Atlanta	147.59	22

[1] Data from Federal Security Agency. Statistical Circular No. 271, May, 1950.

TABLE 70

RECEIPTS FROM STATE OF MARYLAND AND MISCELLANEOUS REVENUES
FOR CALENDAR YEARS, 1948 AND 1949

Source	1948	1949
GRAND TOTAL	$5,365,038.62	$5,313,017.90
Total—From State of Maryland	5,295,812.19	5,191,135.42
Part Payment of Salaries	259,518.70	255,082.65
Federal Vocational Fund	82,868.15	66,047.47
Physically Handicapped Children	10,000.00	6,255.70
Teachers' Pensions	1,157,198.00	955,219.75
Vocational Rehabilitation	3,112.50	3,345.83
Basic Aid per Classroom Unit	1,459,366.67	1,533,400.00
Basic Aid per Pupil	2,053,156.67	2,128,720.00
Incentive Fund for Buildings	260,591.50	216,917.14
Junior College	10,000.00	26,146.88
Total—Miscellaneous Revenues	69,226.43	121,882.48
Tuition—Non-resident Pupils	48,012.75	58,312.42
School Board Revenue	722.78	1,169.93
Intestate Estates Fund	20,490.90	62,400.13

TABLE 71

Financial Report for the Fiscal Year January 1 to December 31, 1948

	RECEIPTS			Cash Expenditures and Accounting Adjustments	DISBURSEMENTS		Total
	Appropriations	Cash Increments and Accounting Adjustments	Total Credits		Forwarded to 1949	Forwarded to City Treasury	
TOTAL	$18,745,099.00	$757,583.86	$19,502,682.86	$19,541,748.26	$39,065.40	....	$19,502,682.86
General Control	439,208.00	151,507.45	590,715.45	590,715.45	....	....	590,715.45
Instructional Service:							
Day Schools	15,140,185.00 a	323,549.57	15,463,734.57	15,504,880.09	41,145.52	....	15,463,734.57
Veterans' Institute	180,485.00	7,906.76	188,391.76	188,391.76	....	....	188,391.76
Night School	275,181.00	....	275,181.00	275,181.00	....	....	275,181.00
Summer School	40,000.00	....	40,000.00	40,000.00	....	....	40,000.00
Operation of Plant	1,890,545.00	137,202.11	2,027,747.11	2,027,747.11	....	....	2,027,747.11
Maintenance of Plant	593,500.00	2,460.04	595,960.04	595,960.04	....	....	595,960.04
Auxiliary Agencies	180,995.00	134,957.93 b	315,952.93	313,872.81	2,080.12	....	315,952.93
Fixed Charges	5,000.00	....	5,000.00	5,000.00	....	....	5,000.00

a Exclusive of operations to liquidate overdraft of $1,350,000.00 from 1947 account teachers' salaries.
b This amount includes $39,510.08 forwarded from 1947.

TABLE 72

FINANCIAL REPORT FOR THE FISCAL YEAR JANUARY 1 TO DECEMBER 31, 1949

	RECEIPTS			DISBURSEMENTS			
	Appropriations	Cash Increments and Accounting Adjustments	Total Credits	Cash Expenditures and Accounting Adjustments	Forwarded To 1950	Forwarded to City Treasury	Total
TOTAL	$22,953,001.50a	$ 211,323.51	$23,164,325.01	$22,720,534.07	$393,796.00	$49,994.94	$23,164,325.01
General Control	562,542.50	14,729.42	577,271.92	570,257.62	2,800.48	4,213.82	577,271.92
Instructional Services:							
Day Schools	18,088,944.00	46,666.34	18,135,610.34	18,009,863.22	111,960.91	13,786.21	18,135,610.34
Veterans'							
Institute	164,700.00	....	164,700.00	164,700.00	....	....	164,700.00
Night School	299,400.00	....	299,400.00	299,400.00	....	....	299,400.00
Summer School	25,000.00	....	25,000.00	25,000.00	....	....	25,000.00
Operation of Plant	2,221,215.00	50,359.20	2,271,574.20	2,248,598.17	22,864.00	112.03	2,271,574.20
Maintenance of Plant	1,304,500.00	46,911.92	1,351,311.92	1,064,885.04	254,544.00	31,882.88	1,351,311.92
Auxiliary Agencies	281,700.00	50,932.48	332,632.48	331,035.98	1,596.50	....	332,632.48
Fixed Charges	5,000.00	1,824.15	6,824.15	6,794.04	30.11	....	6,824.15

a This amount includes $129,000 appropriated from School Board Intestate Estates Fund.

INDEX

INDEX—*Continued*

CPSIA information can be obtained
at www.ICGtesting.com
Printed in the USA
BVHW04*0200230818
525056BV00011BB/692/P